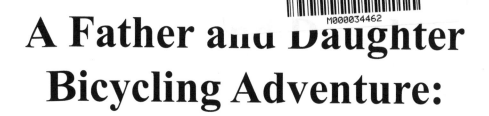

A Father and Daughter Bicycling Adventure:

A Cross-Country Journey and a Six Week Tour of New Zealand's South Island

A Bicycle Launch in Cape Canaveral, Florida
with a Wheel Stop in San Diego, California
Exploring the South Island of New Zealand

Michael A. Rice and Jocelyn M. Rice

A Father and Daughter Bicycling Adventure:
A Cross-Country Journey and a Six Week Tour of New Zealand's South Island
Copyright © 2012 by Michael A. Rice and Jocelyn M. Rice

Cover design and page layout by MagicGraphix.com

ISBN-13: 978-0-9898845-0-1
First edition published 2013

Visit our website
FatherDaughterCyclingAdventures.com

Dedication:

We would like to dedicate this book to all those in this world that are physically unable to ride a bicycle, yet dream of adventure.

I dedicate this book to my late Gramma Polly and Uncle Lynn who showed me what independence, strength, humor, and courage could accomplish. - *Jocelyn*

I dedicate this book to my late mom and dad who let me go and gave me wings to discover this wonderful world and also to my late sister Susan who helped instill independence within me. – *Mike*

Acknowledgments

I would like to thank my father for granting me the opportunity to ride with him, my 'Momster' for being there whenever I needed a pick me up after a long hard ride, my neighbor 'Uncle' Chris for inspiring in me bicycle touring as a way to travel, and my fifth grade teacher, Mr. Smouse for teaching me to never give up on your dreams. I'd also like to acknowledge Matt and Chris at Matt's Bicycle Center in Cocoa Beach, Florida for being friends willing to help with all our bicycle needs. And lastly, I'd like to thank all my friends that have supported me through all my tours thus far. – Jocelyn June 2013

I would to thank my neighbor Chris who's inspiration started us into the bicycle touring lifestyle, all those friendly people across the U.S. and New Zealand who helped us along the way, my sister Tish and brother-in-law Jim who gave us our destination in San Diego, and also to Tish for being our biggest 'cheerleader', Jocelyn who tolerated her slow dad and waited for me to catch up and for being the type of daughter that I could ride day in and day out with and still be best friends, my son Cary who helped take care of the house and made life easier for my wife and my wife Andrea who let me go and live my dreams. – Mike, June 2013

Foreword:

Years ago we toiled away in school and studied many of the great explorers such as the Lewis and Clark expedition, Sir Edmund Hillary climbing Mount Everest and Ernest Shackleton exploring Antarctica. I recall thinking as a young student on what an exciting time it would have been to be part of those exploration teams. Today we still have the thirst for a good exploration challenge. People still reach out to explore on many levels. Some are up on the International Space Station, others are studying science on the South Pole, but many a common man is exploring the continents with backpacking ventures and cycling tours. In the past, I have headed out on my own cycling adventures. Upon my return, I would retell the stories of the challenges and triumphs of the trip. Cycling trips by nature are full of them. Mike Rice and his family live across the street from me. We shared many a meal together and often the stories of the road would be part our conversation. I suspect thoughts of long trips started to cook in the back in Mike's mind. Cycling trips can be like an infectious virus. At first you think about a small trip and then it grows and grows in your mind. It starts to take over your thoughts until the day you hit the road. I recall how Mike updated me on his plans for his solo trip: what to pack, what to leave home, what route to take, and how far to travel each day. He started training with his loaded bike and would head out for a full day of riding in the searing Florida heat. It wasn't a quick loop but rather 60 to 80 miles for a daily training ride. I guess, at this point, I figured that he was serious about this trip. His daughter Jocelyn caught wind of his plans, and being no stranger to cycling, she persuaded Mike to allow her to accompany him. What a wonderful team. They truly compliment each other on this father daughter journey.

I hope their adventure moves you into pursuing your own adventure!
– Chris Ihde, June 2013

"Hills, wind, rain, and bicycle grease are the ingredients for a grand adventure and build character."

– Michael Rice

Contents

Part 1:

United States

Prologue

As I lay on the bike path, with my bike on top of me, I struggled to regain my senses. Jocelyn and I had been in the middle of a good ride from Navarre Beach, Florida to Pensacola Beach when suddenly I fell on the sandy path. I had been attempting to take a picture of the two of us by holding my camera out ahead when a gust of wind pushed me into some deep sand where I lost my balance and tumbled down. Jocelyn, who was drafting me, also fell when her bike hit me on my left side. My right lower leg bled while my left knee throbbed. I looked at Jocelyn and asked if she was okay.

"I'm fine, Dad," she replied, "but you don't look so good."

Great! I thought. All this happened because I was trying to take a picture and was distracted. As I lay there, Jocelyn was able to get up and situated. I struggled to stand but couldn't. A police officer stopped and asked if we needed assistance. He sat in his car the entire time as I was trying to get up, asking Jocelyn about our trip and wanting to hear the details of our adventure. I don't think he wanted to get involved if I was hurt — and I *was* hurt. Jocelyn helped me up while I just kept repeating how stupid I was. My bike appeared to be okay; only the GPS mounted on my aerodynamic bar was beginning to pop off.

Together, Jocelyn and I assessed the situation. My left side hurt terribly as I struggled to breathe. I felt really bad for Jocelyn because it wasn't her fault that she'd hit me. It was all for that stupid picture. It was a real struggle to get back on the bike and continue the ride. The path was uneven, and it hurt to breathe and to sit. I knew there were some condos about a mile ahead. I told Jocelyn that when we got there, I wouldn't be able make it any further and we would need to find a hospital or clinic.

We pulled into the condo parking lot. I barely got off my bike and almost fell again. I walked around for a little bit, trying to find some relief, but I finally sat down on a bench. I wasn't able to move anymore.

A security guard came up and asked if we needed any help. He said the nearest hospital was in Gulfport Breeze, about nine miles away. He also said there was a bridge. I thought about the headwind and my pain and knew there was no way I could make it. He asked me if he should call 911 or just the regular number. I said no to the 911, so Jocelyn and I sat and waited.

Soon a lifeguard truck appeared, towing a jet ski. The two lifeguards helped me up to the truck's tailgate and were soon taking my vitals. I struggled to breathe. I could hardly talk. They brought out an oxygen bottle and asked several questions. The ambulance appeared with a driver and two paramedics. I was worried about my bike, but the lifeguards said they would load it into their truck and deliver it to the hospital for me. They offered to take Jocelyn's bike also, but she said she would ride. The paramedics loaded me on a gurney and into the ambulance. They connected the ambulance oxygen and we took off.

I never got a chance to say anything to Jocelyn, as she had already taken off some time before, but I knew she was feeling real bad.

I lay there on the ambulance gurney, thinking about how I had really messed up our trip. I knew something bad had happened to me inside and that it wasn't going to be a matter of just jumping back on my bike and continuing our adventure. I thought, *Now what?* This was our third day back on our bikes after returning from my dad's funeral in California. I was still very much hurting emotionally from that loss, and now I was physically hurt. It had been hard enough getting back on my bike three days earlier, with my only motivation being my dad's last words to me. Those words had gotten me back in the saddle. What would be my motivation now?

At that moment, I saw what I will forever remember as one of my saddest visions. We passed Jocelyn, pedaling toward the hospital. I saw her face and started to cry. The paramedics tried to calm me down. I couldn't talk anymore. Instead, I could only look back on how I'd gotten here.

Chapter 1:
Pre-launch Preps and Training

My family and I have had a good life living beachside in Cape Canaveral, Florida. I have worked as an electrical engineer with the Space Shuttle Program at Kennedy Space Center for the better part of 30 years, while my wife Andee has taught at the local elementary school. We have raised two children, Cary and Jocelyn. The recreation choices are boundless here, from anything at the beach or on the water to miles and miles of flat roads.

Bike riding has always been second nature to all of us. It wasn't until eight years ago that we decided to upgrade from our standard beach cruisers to bikes that we could put a few miles on. After Jocelyn got a new one, I decided that the time was good for me too, so I bought a Raleigh SC30 for $250. I started riding it around town and ventured down into Cocoa Beach. For the most part, I am a jogger and did that to stay in reasonable shape, but sore knees had me rethinking my jogging, so I decided to ride more for fitness instead of just around town.

One Sunday morning, I rode to the Officer's Club Beach at Patrick Air Force Base. The distance was 12 miles, and I thought, *This is great!* I was so proud of my 24 mile ride and so was Andee. The following Sunday, I did even more. This went on for a few years, and I really enjoyed these rides. Sometimes the kids went with me, but usually I was a loner. I noticed many others riding much faster than I, so I tried to go faster but was continually passed. After discussing this with my biker co-workers, I realized that maybe it was the 26" wheel size and wide tires. I went to the local bike shop and asked about faster tires. The owner just looked at me and said, "It isn't about the tires; you just need to pedal harder." I guess I didn't know much about bicycle riding.

Through all this, my neighbor, Chris, would regale us about his bike touring trips throughout the country. He has been up and down the West and East Coasts and parts in-between. Chris was a real touring guy. So

I started thinking that maybe it is not about going faster, as in all the roadies who always pass me, but in wanting to go longer distances. Now I was waking up earlier and earlier on Sunday mornings to ride, and I was basically leaving for the day. That didn't go over well with Andee, but the first time I rode to Sebastian Inlet and crossed the bridge, I was hooked on distance. My distance that day was 84 miles. I was so stoked and proud. The years passed by and I eventually added Saturdays to my routine. Andee didn't like my being gone on the weekends, but she still supported me in my interest. Jocelyn was away at college in North Carolina, and Cary was working in Tallahassee after graduating from Florida State University. The Space Shuttle Program was winding down, and I was working four, ten-hour days a week. I was getting all the housework done on Fridays and spending my weekends on the road.

Since I had a Kennedy Space Center badge, I was able to bike north through Cape Canaveral Air Force Station and exit north through the Space Center. I did this whenever there was a north wind blowing, as I preferred having the wind at my back on the homeward trek. I had a variety of routes going north, south, and west toward Orlando. For each ride, I packed lots of water along with some energy gels and a peanut butter and jelly sandwich. It's funny, but up to this point I had never thought of touring. I was just riding and riding. It was just fun, unless the weather didn't cooperate or I picked the wrong direction to go. But soon I figured out that maybe headwinds build character, so I rode harder and harder. I was riding several thousand miles a year.

By the end of 2010, we all realized that the shuttle program really was going to end — probably in May of 2011. I distinctly remember a December 2010 ride to Daytona Beach. I was on my way home when it hit me. I was tired of just going home all the time after my long rides, so why not go somewhere? I was going to be unemployed soon, so it had to be grand. I thought about several destinations, but one by one I scratched them off my list. I needed a big trip, one that would give me something to reach for.

Then it hit me: Cross country seemed to be big enough. San Diego sounded great, and my sister Tish and brother-in-law Jim live in Pacific Beach. I decided, "That's where I want to go!" But then came more questions. When? Summertime may be too hot. How long will it take? As I pedaled, I did some quick calculations. I figured it would take maybe two months. And then — Bingo! I had been flying out at Thanksgiving time to visit my mom and dad in Oxnard, California for many years. My mom had passed away in 2008, but I had continued to go out to visit Dad. While there, we would usually drive down to Tish and Jim's house in San Diego and visit for several days. So how about if I left Florida in mid-September and rode to San Diego in time for Thanksgiving? Jim could drive up to Oxnard and pick up Dad, and we could all have Thanksgiving together as usual. Mentally, my plan was in place. To me it sounded like a grand trip. As I neared home, I wondered how to approach Andee with this grand plan.

I didn't say anything right away. I thought I had better do some research first. The best place to start was with my neighbor, Chris. He gave me some touring basics and several websites to check out. One of these was crazyguyonabike.com. He said to be careful though, because one can get lost for hours on that website, and he was right. I read many journals about people riding the Southern Tier, which is basically from St. Augustine to San Diego. Chris even brought out his Adventure Cycling Association Southern Tier maps. I studied everything more and more, thinking, *Hey, I'm an engineer, and I have worked all my life thinking and rethinking stuff.* There are people who would hop on their bike the next day and just go — but not me. When I'm thinking and planning, I get pretty quiet. So during all my thinking, planning, and silence, Andee eventually figured out that something was going on.

I finally told her of my grand plan. She gave me a blank stare and asked, "So… what dog are you going to take?" And then it was, "How are you going to pay for this?" Well, that part was easy. At layoff, my company would pay me my unused sick leave. Since I was hardly ever sick, I was looking at around $10,000. I figured if I couldn't ride cross country for less than that, there is a real problem. Andee eventually agreed that it was a great idea. So now I had to find a new bike… or so I thought.

I diligently researched the Internet and looked at many different kinds of bikes, from road, hybrids, and touring. I knew that I wanted straight handlebars, as the drop bars are uncomfortable for me. My Raleigh is a hybrid, so I wanted to stay away from that to keep the mountain part out. I read that the fork shock absorbers would be uncomfortable for such a long trip and actually can slow you down. There are so many touring bikes that I was confused. But I liked that they all came with braze-ons (attach points) for racks and water bottle cages. And the plus is that touring bikes are built for the extra weight I was going to carry. I wanted to camp, so I was planning on carrying 60 pounds total on the rear and front panniers. I visited several bike shops and told them about my plans.

Through my research and sharing, I decided that the Surly Long Haul Trucker was it. The tubing is double-walled in thickness; all the braze-on attach points that one needs are there; it comes in straight or drop handle bars, and the price was right. I visited Matt at my local bike shop, Matt's Bicycle Center, and talked with him since I hadn't stopped by there yet. I told him my plan and asked him what bike I should get, and he answered, "The Surly Long Haul Trucker!" Bingo! Both Matt and I had come up with the same bike!

As I continued to ride my Raleigh, I said to myself, "What is wrong with this bike? I know it really well and it rides good. It is not fast (It has slow tires!), but it has gotten me everywhere I have wanted to go. It is very heavy at 35 pounds, so it can pretty much carry anything." On one of my southward rides to Vero Beach, I stopped by Matt's again on my way home. I asked him if this Raleigh could make it to California. He hemmed and hawed, looked it over some, and said, "Sure it will… with some overhaul." Right then I decided to ride my Raleigh and told Matt I would bring it in for an overhaul. I was getting excited now because I had my vehicle!

I dropped my bike off a week later. Matt changed out all the cables and brakes, installed a new rear gear, and replaced the chain. He also trued both wheels. Now came the fun part — outfitting my Raleigh. This took more and more research on racks, panniers, lights, etc., and of course a new saddle as my current one was not that comfortable. I was expecting daily rides of 60-70 miles, so this was a very important decision. After purchasing several saddles at local shops and online, and five returns later, I settled on the Brooks B-67 leather saddle. It was as comfortable on the

100th mile as it was on the first. There is a break-in time for this saddle, but mine was good to go. I didn't like the Raleigh seat tube, so Matt found a mountain biking one that can be adjusted for a softer or harder ride.

The racks and panniers were another research adventure. I wanted tough racks that could carry a good amount of weight and not break. I had read in several journals about racks breaking and the biker having to find a town with a welder, which isn't as easy as it sounds. For the panniers I wanted something totally waterproof. Once again I had read stories of so-called waterproof panniers that had soaked through in a heavy rain. I chose Tubus stainless steel racks for front and rear and Ortlieb panniers. Both of these items are made in Germany and have quite a reputation. Tubus also sold adaptor hardware for installation on bikes without attach points, and as my Raleigh didn't have any, this worked out well. The racks and panniers were very easy to install, and I was really impressed by the quality. I did spend around $600 for all, but it was well worth it. By the way, that's $350 more than I paid for the Raleigh!

And then the training began!

I started out with a gallon of water in all four panniers, which added 30 pounds. I really felt the extra load and was now riding even slower. But that was good, because it made me train harder. My rear would each fit another gallon, so I added another 15 pounds, which brought it up to 45 pounds for water. I had also been purchasing and adding more equipment. Matt turned me on to a cool aerodynamic bar which enabled me to lean over and stretch out occasionally. It was basically like riding with drop bars, but I was more easily able to move back upright. I then researched and purchased a Garmin GPS which came with the perfect mount that I installed on the aerodynamic bar. The GPS was attached right at the end, allowing a perfect view of the GPS. Installed in the GPS was the North American street maps micro SD card. Along with new light and excellent side mirrors, I was really looking good — or so I thought.

One of my typical rides was to head south over the Sebastian Inlet Bridge and onto North Vero Beach. It is about 100 miles round trip. During the weekends, there are many roadies riding hard from Ocean Avenue in Melbourne Beach to the Sebastian Inlet Bridge and back. It is a fast and flat 30 mile round trip ride. As I was riding along one day, two women rode by and one said, "Have you noticed how many old beater guys are out today?" The other just laughed. I took that as an insult and tried to catch up with them, but I soon realized that, "This old beast will not catch them!" I can't remember if I was referring to myself or to the bike, but that is when I started calling my bike, "The Beast." It certainly looked like one with all the stuff on it. The Beast was heavy, but I was on a mission. Little did I realize that the cost of the preparations would now double.

Jocelyn was close to completing her second year at Western Carolina University in North Carolina, where she was attending on a track and field scholarship for her discus throwing ability. She had been the high school discus champion for the State of Florida in 2009, but because of coaching changes and indecision about what she wanted to major in, she decided to leave WCU at the end of the semester. Andee told her my plans, and Jocelyn immediately said, "I want to go," and at that moment, my efforts and dollars doubled.

Her old Mongoose bike would definitely not make the journey. The trip would be easier with two of us as there would always be someone to watch the bikes while one went into a store or restroom. The bikes could easily be locked but not all the panniers with our gear. The bike solution was very simple. We went to Matt's and had Jocelyn measured out for a new — you guessed it — the Surly Long Haul Trucker. The bike I was going to get!

A few weeks later the Surly arrived. What a beautiful riding machine! I looked back and forth between The Beast and the Surly several times and just shook my head. Matt did size it and added some neck tubing, just in case it defaulted to me. It was also easy to fit out. I just ordered everything I did for The Beast, including an aerodynamic bar, Brook's saddle, Tubus racks, Ortlieb panniers, lights, etc. The Surly had all the attach points for the racks so it was extremely easy to install. Matt also installed a set of fenders on The Beast as the Surly came with them installed. Fenders are very important and really make for an easy cleanup after riding though the rain. Now we had two fully-equipped bikes loaded with 45 pounds of water each and several more pounds in bike gear. I know we wanted to camp, but since we had never done that, I was thinking how to put more gear on the bikes. We needed a tent, sleeping bags, ground pads, etc. At this point I was thinking that this was getting ridiculous. We were going to max out somewhere! Research began on lightweight camping gear. I soon discovered that this was a whole different animal.

We went to an outside/camping store in Orlando. The salespeople were very friendly and informative. I had done some research and came specifically to look at the MSR Hubba-Hubba two person tents. We met a girl there who had used one for years and liked the quick and easy setup, plus the tent is very light. It also received high ratings from the many cycling adventure websites I had researched. That was easy, so then we picked out two self-inflating pads and a few other odds and ends. Amazon took care of the rest of the camping gear. I also bought two more waterproof duffel bags from Ortlieb to store everything. People laughed at me when I bought a collapsible vinyl water bucket to do laundry, but it turned out to be very useful.

The last space shuttle flight landed in July of 2011. Two weeks later I was out the door. I had been very fortunate to have had such an interesting and varied 35 years of work, but now I was ready for a new adventure.

Jocelyn and I did several "dress rehearsal" rides that included everything for the trip except for clothes and other things that were to be packed in the panniers that still held water jugs. At this point, whenever we stopped to refill water and such, people asked us the typical questions like, "Where are you from?" and, "Where are you headed?" After all, we were fully loaded. I got used to blurting out, "On a cross-country training run from Cape Canaveral and now going home."

I remember stopping in a park one day, and a little kid asking his mom if I was a bum. I weighed all my stuff (with the water jugs) and it came to 76 pounds. What a beast! No wonder I was getting tired so quickly. I was also riding 3-4 days in a row. My daily mileage was down to 80. No sense pushing it. The August Florida heat was brutal. I would stop at beachfront parks to take head showers. During this time I also moved up the date from the last week in September to a departure on September 6th, just in case we needed more time to get to San Diego. For a number of reasons, this turned out to be a very wise move.

I was also riding west to River Drive in Rockledge/Cocoa for some hill work. Nothing really impressive was there as far as size, so I just went back and forth over the many small hills as I needed some kind of hill training. Central Florida does not lend itself to training for long grades or mountains. For my last big training run, I rode five days and 310 miles with full gear. I loaded and unloaded each day. The loading got easier and easier. The Tubus racks and Ortlieb panniers are super easy to work with. On one of my last rides, I was passed by two guys from California headed to the beach. One of them yelled, "Almost there!" I later saw a newspaper article about a father and son biking from Huntington Beach, California.

Jocelyn was on a different schedule, so we hadn't really done any long rides together. She was training in her own way. I was a bit concerned about this as Chris had told me that if you can ride 3-4 days in a row without saddle pain then you should do okay.

I had bought a Samsung Galaxy Pad to upload pictures and a daily journal to *crazyguyonabike.com*. I tried really hard to get used to the touchscreen, but in the end it was just too complicated to do everything I wanted it to do, so I decided to pack my 13-inch laptop. I was used to it and it was very easy to do daily updates. I also purchased a MiFi through Verizon so that I could connect to the Internet wherever there was a cellular signal. This proved to work out well since most of the WiFi spots were so slow.

We took our bikes to Matt's for a last tune-up and for maintenance instructions. Matt was very helpful and thorough. He found a crack on my front wheel and ordered a new one. The last few days were spent packing and unpacking three times. We had everything set out in the living room on two tables. It all had to fit somewhere. Chris came over and stared at the mess. He would say, "What's that for? What's that for?" many times. He eventually walked away, shaking his head, and said, "You'll learn."

On September 5, I thought, "Tomorrow is the day." Sadly, that night my sister called me and said that Dad was not doing well. His caregiver and the local parish deacon were trying to get him to go to the hospital. He had been in and out of the hospital several times the past few years and was tired of it all. At 89, he had a right to be. He was still sharp as a tack, but his body was giving out. I called him and tried to talk him into going to the hospital, but he refused. I told him that we could postpone the trip and I could fly out to California the next day to see him. He knew about our upcoming adventure and was very adamant with, "No! You and Jocelyn start your trip, and I will be with you all the way. Keep those wheels going round and round."

I told Dad that we would start the bike ride. He then thanked me for being the son that I was and I thanked him for being a wonderful father. I told him I would see him in San Diego in two months. His reply was, "No... this is it."

I don't remember getting any sleep that night. The bikes were fully loaded and sitting in the garage. They were ready to have their rear tires dipped in the Atlantic Ocean, about 600 feet away. But I wasn't ready at all. I was a mess wondering what to do.

Mike

Jocelyn

"It is by riding a bicycle that you learn the contours of a country best, since you have to sweat up the hills and coast down them. Thus you remember them as they actually are, while in a motor car only a high hill impresses you, and you have no such accurate remembrance of country you have driven through as you gain by riding a bicycle."

– Ernest Hemingway

Chapter 2:
We Have Launched into our Mission and Cleared Cape Canaveral

Day 1: A Great Start But with a Heavy Heart
Tuesday, September 6, 2011: 83 miles –
Total so Far: 83 miles

The departure day had finally arrived. Throughout the night, I had wrestled with the idea of flying out to see my dad. But he was very insistent that we start our trip. I decided to respect his wishes and start our father and daughter adventure. We were up with the sun and pedaled the 600 feet to the beach. We walked our bikes across the beach to the Atlantic.

What a tough beginning — walking a fully-loaded bike across the sand! I had weighed everything the night before. Jocelyn's Surly was 27 pounds, and she was carrying 55 pounds plus her weight. My Raleigh was 35 pounds with 65 pounds of stuff. I say "stuff" because it was way too much. But what do you do? Fortunately, during the training I had lost 35 pounds, so my combined weight with shoes and hydration pack was 210 pounds. So my bike totaled 310 pounds! Wow! I decided to not add up Jocelyn's.

The surf and wind had subsided from the last several days of Hurricane Katia. Katia had passed well offshore over the weekend, and Jocelyn, my son Cary, and I had taken the time to enjoy our last surfing excursion for a while. We felt envious of Cary because our real hurricane season was just starting and he would score much more surf in the upcoming two months. We walked our bikes into the water and posed for pictures with several of the neighbors. We stayed too long and sank into the sand. Now our shoes and socks were wet! We quickly left and met everyone on the dune crossover to say our goodbyes. We rode past a large banner that Andee had made, and one of our neighbors turned on her hose and sprayed our wheels as we passed by. The wheels were full of salt and sand, so we stopped at our house and washed them as well as changed our wet socks. As we rode out of the neighborhood, I zeroed out the GPS.

The weather threatened thunderstorms as we looked north. Between that and wondering what our future held, I had plenty on my mind. How was my dad doing? Would I see him again? When we would be home again? Would we complete the journey? Would we have a safe trip? Would Andee and Cary be okay for these next few months? When you are traveling on a bike, there is plenty of time to think.

We took the north route through the visitor's area of Kennedy Space Center and stopped for some pictures at the space shuttle mock-up "Inspiration". I figured we would need some of that. Our first rest stop was in Titusville on US 1. We both took a potty break and had an apple. As we continued north, a hard headwind blew in some nasty-looking weather. A friend of mine from work had his sailboat in dry dock at the local boatyard, so we decided to see if he was home and maybe we could get out of the impending weather. I banged on the side of his Westsail 32 and Scott appeared. While Jocelyn watched the bikes, Scott and I drove to a local store for sandwiches. We returned and he grabbed a few beers from the boat. We ate in a covered dockside pavilion. It was a momentous occasion, as I exclaimed, "My first beer of the trip. Thanks, Scott!"

After an hour, the weather had cleared and we fairly flew to Daytona on a strong southwest wind. Our goal that day was to camp at Tomoka State Park. As we rode through South Daytona, with the light rapidly disappearing, we decided on a motel instead as it was another 15 miles to the park and we didn't want to ride in the dark. We settled on a somewhat decent motel where the clerk thought we were police because of the bright clothes we were wearing. The small room was $40 and we navigated our bikes inside. Then the fun began. Where was all the laundry stuff? Where was the... etc., etc, etc? We literally took everything off the bikes and emptied all the panniers looking for stuff. What a mess! There had to be a better way. But hey, we were beginners. At that point, I biked to a local gas station and purchased a 6-pack of beer. When I returned, we had a wonderful cold beer and did our laundry in the collapsible vinyl bucket. Chris had suggested doing the laundry in the sink or bathtub. We found the bucket method easier and more efficient. The actual bike riding was just part of the work, and all the other work such as laundry, eating, and updating websites entailed much more. With the clean laundry strung throughout the room on a clothesline, we went next door to Porkie's BBQ for a delicious pulled-pork sandwich and a draft Yuengling beer. It was a good first day followed by a great night's sleep.

Jocelyn: It is almost ten at night and I am pretty much exhausted. Today was our departure day! With a 7:00 A.M. launch time, my father and I had a good send-off from most of the neighbors, my mother, and my brother. I live about 600 feet from the Atlantic Ocean on the East Coast of Florida, in the land of the space shuttle farm. It is a beautiful small beach town that is unique in many ways. As we peddled down to the beach to dip our rear tires into the Atlantic, I couldn't quite grasp all the emotions I was feeling. I'm pretty sure it was every emotion known to mankind, if that's even possible. My hands were clammy, and my body was shaky. Little droplets of water slipped away from my blue eyes and ran down underneath my sunglasses. I automatically felt the urge to have to go to the restroom again, which truthfully I had gone five times before finally leaving my house. Yes, I am a little nervous. We will be gone for almost two months. I found myself already replaying images of the good-bye hugs and kisses my amazing dog gave me. I miss her already. Her name is Yaki and she is my princess. As we reached the beach, I never thought that walking through the sand with a loaded bicycle would be such tough work. Both my father and I are carrying almost sixty pounds of equipment. Such things as sleeping bags, a tent, clothing, towels, toiletries, sunscreen, extra tire tubes, extra heavy-duty touring tires, a tool box, one cooler, extra shoes, covers for our bikes when it rains, some food, and a computer and journal. I've not mentioned quite a few supplies, but you get the gist. Dipping our rear tires in the Atlantic is a ritual for all cyclists who are about to embark on such an adventure as riding their bicycles across the country. Slightly misjudging the tide and the roaring waves, both of our feet pretty much got baptized. *Great!* I thought. *Just what we need, soggy, wet feet on the very first day of the trip.* But the wind and surf were rough from Hurricane Katia. After many pictures were taken by my family and the neighbors, we began the trudge back through the soft, white sand.

My mother surprised us with a long banner, wishing us off to the great journey ahead. I hopped off my bike one more time to give everyone hugs; just one more from my mom was really all I wanted. We rode up my street and out onto the major road of A1A. If you have ever been on this road, it really isn't major, but it is the main road connecting all the towns on the outer barrier island where I have lived my entire life. In an instant, I heard a honk and thought to myself, *This might be a reoccurring sound we will hear on this ride.* I looked into my mirror and saw my mother waving and taking more pictures — typical loving mom I'd say. She made me smile, as she usually always does. My mom and I are sisters at heart and even more so after I pledged her same sorority my freshman year of college, almost two years ago. I love her so much, although we might bicker, but we're truthful and always want the best out of each other. I miss her already. I just hope she will do okay without either me or my dad there. Yes, she has my brother and now three dogs, but I know her and I know she will miss me. We hang out a lot when she isn't stressing about her schoolwork or teaching. She is so inspiring, a hard worker, and one of the socially bubbliest people I know. Yup, I just decided that maybe I should stop talking about my mother, as it just makes me miss her even more. This will be a long road for all the memories I do have, the people I miss, the events I remember, and the life-changing experiences I have faced. I look forward to the mental aspect of this ride.

We headed north on a route we have taken many times before while training. Right away my dad and I hit headwinds, which is odd because when we were at the beach dipping our tires into the ocean, the wind was in our favor. I learned rather quickly that the winds can either be your best friend, or your enemy. The weather, as we suspected, began to threaten us just as we reached Titusville. My father made the decision to stop at a local marina to grab some lunch. We surprisingly ran into one of his work friends. He was there preparing for an adventure himself with his sailboat. Scott, his friend, had the honor of giving my father his first beer of the trip. I say that is honorable just because my dad is a big beer drinker and always has been. When I was little, we used to have a really neat bar in our house. It was rather huge, but maybe it just seemed that way since I was definitely smaller than I am now. I remember being my dad's bartender, pouring him a pint, and pouring myself a shot of his favorite beer, Budweiser. That's how I rolled. So I'll be the first to tell you: Beer drinking is just one of the hobbies I picked up from my father, even though I legally can't drink yet. The rain and gusty winds cleared, and we fairly flew north with a southwest wind to Daytona Beach, Florida. Earlier, we'd mapped out where we wanted to end our first day of riding, but unfortunately we didn't make it to Tomoka State Park to camp like we'd planned. So we settled for a "decent" motel in South Daytona. After almost 83 miles, we both really needed a bed and a hot shower. We were hoping, though, to camp some. I mean, after all, we were carrying the equipment for it!

During the ride that first day, I decided to mentally tally random things along this journey across the country. The thought came to me after riding over the third bridge of the day that I was going to try and keep track of how many bridges we rode over. How many times I accidentally ran over previously run-over road kill, although I must admit it is gross. But sometimes some random carcass just appears out of nowhere and then, "Bammm!" or rather, "Squish?" Let's hope that number doesn't increase often. Another thing I am going to tally is going to be how many times I happen to run my bike off the road. I think maybe I should pay attention more. I just cannot help that I love to look around and be aware of my surroundings. I wanted to take in all the scenery, from the road to the beautiful sky and stars. So far the tally is:

9 Bridges, 2 Road Kill, 2 Run-offs.

Well, I think this is a good first journal entry. Let us all pray that my father and I find some good yummy dinner and get some good sleep. Tomorrow is day two! In the words of my grandma, "Good night to all the ships at sea."

"Surprised we got this far." Mike.

"Puts us in a good perspective." Jocelyn.

Dipping our rear tires in the Atlantic Ocean

Day 2: When Did Jocelyn Become a Bike Roadie?
Wednesday, September 7th, 2011; 57 miles –
Total so far: 140 miles

We had a good night's sleep and were repacked and out of the room by 8:00 A.M. Riding through Daytona was not fun at all, as rush hour was in full effect. When I had removed my front panniers the night before, I had noticed that a nut and spacer had loosened and fallen off the front rack. We stopped at a local Ace Hardware store where I purchased replacement hardware, and we were soon on our way. After a nerve-racking morning ride, we stopped off at a small restaurant in Ormond Beach for a delicious stack of pancakes. It was funny that I went through our preplanned routine of removing the Ortlieb rear purse, which contained our valuables, and locked both bikes together with two 10-foot cable combination locks. After doing this, we walked inside and sat right next to the window. Jocelyn gave me that look like, "What did we just go through all that for, Dad?" That's just me.

After breakfast, we continued into Bunnell and then Palatka. The road had good, smooth shoulders with lots of shady pine trees. I thought, *This is what country riding is all about!* The first of many logging trucks rushed by us, carrying long, skinny pine trees. And believe me, they do not slow down. We would learn to really dislike these trucks in the weeks to come. I soon noticed that Jocelyn was riding way ahead of me. She would then pull over and wait, and as soon as I caught up she would start again. *It must be the Surly with faster tires,* I thought. But then, it was probably her youth. She hadn't trained as much as I had, but she was kicking my butt! She was even slowing down and then passing me on bridges while looking back at me and smiling. I'd always thought that I would be in front. *We shall see,* I thought.

Soon, we arrived in West Palatka after a beautiful crossing of the St. Johns River. It was around 4:00 P.M., so we pulled over to look at our options. The GPS showed a state park that we called, but there was no camping and no one around. We still had plenty of time to use our 25 pounds of camping gear! So it was another motel. This one was in a seedy area, but there wasn't much else available. According to the Adventure Cycling Association (ACA) map, there weren't any accommodations for another 22 miles. The problem with this motel was there were no bottom floor rooms available. The clerk said we could put our bikes in the maid's storage room. I looked at it and it seemed secure, so we once again removed everything from the bikes. All of this was hauled upstairs and spread out. As we put the bikes in this room I had a funny feeling, so I locked them with both cables to a metal shelf that was bolted onto a wall. As we left, the clerk closed and locked the door.

The first order of the evening was a quick trip to the corner store for beer. Since there was no refrigerator, I also bought a bag of ice. Being smart — or as some would say, "Packing too much unnecessary stuff" — I had brought along my soft beach cooler that holds 12 drinks. It strapped beautifully to the back of Jocelyn's bike. And yes, there were lots of times that we didn't finish the beer and she carried it! What a daughter! Our laundry and other routines were started, and then we walked to a local fast-food place for a sandwich. As I finished updating my website and my last beer, I thought, *This is great! Not a care in the world!* Or so I thought.

Jocelyn: Day two! My dad let me sleep in some, so I was well rested and ready to charge on my bike. My bike's name is Surly, on account of that's its legit name — Surly Long Haul Trucker (LHT). I am pretty much in love with it. It is a beautiful blue with a drop-down handlebar. I have Ortlieb front and rear panniers and both of our sleeping bags. Oh, and I cannot forget the cooler! I like the setup, and I like how my dad and I look together too. I don't think my dad notices, but I am trying to match him in the same clothing color. We seem to get a lot of attention when we are riding and even when we aren't! I like it. I don't know if my dad does because he doesn't like to talk much, just not a social individual. My mom and dad are total opposites when it comes to that. But this morning when my dad checked us out from the motel, the front desk lady apparently told my dad that she thought we were cops, or some professional riding team. We're doing surprisingly well together, and I am trying my hardest to impress him. We've had our ups and downs for the past seven years, since I started high school. Just a lot of issues arose of who I was becoming, like he felt like he'd lost his 'best friend', which in a way he did.

Riding through Daytona during rush hour was an experience, but not a lot of fun. It was rather nerve racking honestly. At one point I yelled up to my dad and said, "I just want to get out of this city!" He hasn't been able to hear me well. I don't know if that is because he is lost in his mind or if he actually can't hear me. Because I know for sure I will be getting lost within my mind on this trip, as it already has happened several times. For a whole hour today all I could think about was ice. I love ice. I used to call it my favorite food, but an ice-cold beverage sounded and still sounds amazing. While riding, I carry three water bottles in the middle of the frame. It is rather warm water at the moment. And I have a neon-green camel back, but I have found that I don't drink a lot from it because it just gets so hot while sitting on my back. The heat has been intense ever since we left the storms yesterday in Titusville. My thermometer on my bicycle stem was hitting just over 95 degrees F. Oh, how I love the hot sun in Florida! I am not being sarcastic either; I really love sunshine in my life.

We continued northwest and flew through Bunnell to Palatka. For lunch we stopped at a gas station and split a cold sandwich. Talk about a good eats. I also got the delicious energy drink Cocaine. Made me feel limitless. That feeling and a bicycle made me rage. This past summer my motto was Rage Hard. I use it in everything that I do, from working out to dancing or surfing, even working! I believe that you should go the hardest possible in anything you do, because then you can say that you did your best — right? So I go hard.

I ended up reaching just over 20 mph. That might not seem fast, but on flat land and with 60 pounds of equipment, I'd say it is. I literally could feel my heart pounding out of my chest. My dad said a few times that I got so far ahead of him that he couldn't even see me! I probably was a few miles ahead of him then. So, you could say I was kicking his butt! I passed him going up a bridge and gave him a big grin, and all he said was, "Showoff." The bridge wasn't that high, but it was our first challenge. My dad barely made it up, which kind of makes me nervous because we will be riding through hills and mountain passes reaching as much as 5,000 feet. He might be walking more than he thinks.

The town we stopped at wasn't the best of towns. The motel happened to have the whole bottom floor as smoking rooms only, which caused a dilemma. We needed a bottom room because we have our bikes, but my dad wasn't about to stay in a smoking room. Putting trust in the manager's advice, we put both bikes in the maid's storeroom. My dad locked them together and we watched the manager lock the door. I had a funny feeling appear and just hoped they would be okay there. After showering and hand washing our clothes, we walked down the street to the local Wendy's and had chili for dinner. I saw some interesting but strange people wandering the streets.

So ready to jump into bed and sleep. My legs hurt some today, more so my quads. My neighbor, Chris, who happens to be a cyclist himself, said that after the third day of riding your body gets used to the constant movement and that your appetite is through the roof. The best thing is that you can eat whatever you like! I am going to enjoy that aspect. I am always trying to diet and watch my weight. My weight tends to bounce around a lot, so I am excited to see the transformation through this crazy form of exercise.

"You'll never see me in this town again!" Mike.

"You can't even see the people walking down the street!" Jocelyn.

Day 3: "The Hills are Alive with the Sound of... Clanking Chains!" Thursday September 8, 2011; 58 miles – Total so Far: 198 miles

I awoke around 4:00 A.M. with a gut feeling of, *Why did we not bring our bikes upstairs?* The motel clerk seemed pretty adamant about not wanting them in the room but had also used the excuse that there were no rooms available on the bottom floor. We were up pretty late and never did see anyone downstairs. Jocelyn had mentioned that this place seemed like a drug dealer's hangout from looking at some of the characters. There were a lot of people hanging around. I just kept thinking that this was a setup to steal our bikes. Wouldn't that be a shocker — trip over after 2 days!

I couldn't get back to sleep. I got up and walked around the parking lot a few times, but it seemed okay. At 7:00 A.M., I rang and rang the buzzer at the office, and the clerk finally appeared from a second-floor room. I told him we would like our bikes now. He said he would be down soon. I woke Jocelyn up and told her we needed to leave. We packed, hauled everything downstairs, and waited until the clerk finally arrived to unlock the storage door. He stood outside while I went in.

The bikes were there, but there was a rear door that I hadn't noticed before. It was completely open! The bikes had been moved, but fortunately my locking method had kept them together and well-cabled to the metal shelf. I had also stripped the bikes to their racks. What a relief! I still think of that morning often. I moved the bikes outside. Jocelyn was watching all our gear, as I didn't trust this place at all. The motel clerk looked sort of surprised as I wheeled them out. We loaded the bikes, and I left the key by the office window. On the way out of town, we stopped at a McDonald's and had breakfast. I told Jocelyn about the attempted burglary of our bikes and that under no circumstances would we ever not have them in our room again. If a motel insisted on them not being in a room, we would look elsewhere. That was our wakeup call.

The day was beautiful but hot. We were finally headed west on Hwy 100, which had been recently repaved with a wide shoulder. There were trees lining both sides, affording us ample shade. Jocelyn noticed all these dark spots between the trees, so we investigated. There were huge spider webs and spiders everywhere. We took several pictures. I got too close to them and Jocelyn said I'd better back off. I had never seen such an array of webbing and huge spiders. After about 20 miles the hills began! It was up and down and rolling. Jocelyn was still riding ahead of me. Nothing seemed to slow her down as I struggled. She even had two beers in the cooler that we hadn't drunk last night!

I finally saw her way ahead and stopped with a long line of cars. Traffic was down to one lane for roadwork. When I caught up with her, I said, "Well, at least somebody can stop you." The guy holding the stop sign laughed.

We soon took off and she shot ahead. A few miles later, my GPS beeped to make a turn as we were headed to Gainesville per the ACA map. I stopped for the turn and could barely see Jocelyn going up another hill. Now what? I turned on my phone and tried calling her several times until she finally answered.

"Where are you, Dad?" she asked.

"Turn around, Jocelyn," I answered.

She finally backtracked to me and said, "You mean I wasted all that energy to go up that big hill?"

"Yes you did!" I replied. We continued on and she stayed closer since I had the maps and GPS. Thank goodness for the cell phone service!

The hills continued and so did the learning of how to continually shift. My bike wasn't used to this, so I sort of clanked along. Of course, Jocelyn just rode quietly along but kept looking at my bike and wondering what I was doing. "Dad, I'm not shifting, so why are you?" she asked. Youth!

We came upon a feed store, Shiloh Feed and Seed, in the middle of nowhere that had a beer sign on it! It was one of those old-looking places you just have to stop at. We went inside and purchased a beer for me and a soda for Jocelyn. I asked the proprietor if I could drink it outside and he said, "Why not?" He came outside and talked with us, and I mentioned all the hills. He looked at me funny and said, "Heck, you ain't seen no hills yet." I would hear that about hills and mountains for the rest of the trip.

We followed the ACA route to the Gainesville-Hawthorne State Bicycle Trail, which was a really fun 15 mile ride. There were small hills and lots of switchbacks that eventually led to Gainesville close to the University of Florida. Jocelyn and I were having so much fun that we started racing. During this ride, we went by a fenced-in middle school. There were several girls hanging out by the fence who asked us if we wanted some heroin or other drugs. I was shocked to say the least! We thought it was very bizarre, as they acted like they were in prison. I told them that I was already high.

"On what?" they asked.

"On riding my bike!" I yelled back. That is so strange for that age.

We met a University of Florida student on the trail who guided us to Gainesville's original water springs, complete with bathroom and a cold-water drinking fountain. "The only one around!" he boasted. What a score! We eventually left the trail and searched for a campsite using the GPS. There were none close by, so we searched for a motel. The first one we came upon looked pretty seedy as we watched two guys lighting a barbeque outside their room under an overhang. We continued on until we saw a Holiday Inn. I went in to get a room and asked where the school was. The desk clerk just stared at me until I finally said, "UF."

She continued to stare at me and answered, "Across the street."

Feeling like a fool, I said, "Never been here."

As we brought the bikes in, she called out to me and said, "Oh, Mr. Rice... you really *are* on bikes. Let me get you a larger room."

That was nice of her. After we did the usual after-ride work, we went out for dinner. Sure enough, across the street was a huge UF sign. After dinner we walked around the football stadium. Fun day!

Jocelyn: Last night, both my dad and I had trouble sleeping, so we got a later start. I know that I had scary nightmares; I just can't remember much. My dad said he, too, woke up several times throughout the night, worried about the bikes most likely, as was I. We actually only got a late start because the manager wouldn't wake up, or at least come out to the office when we rang the bell. He finally came scurrying in with his bed hair and shirt half tucked in after twenty minutes of waiting for him. Talk about a horrible gut feeling; all I could think about was how I really hoped the bikes were still there. When we went into the maintenance room, the bikes were there, but the rear door, which we hadn't even noticed the day before, was completely slung open! The sun shined through the door frame onto our bikes. From that point on we vowed to never, ever, leave the bikes again.

Finally leaving the motel, we stopped at McDonald's right outside of Palatka. I haven't eaten here in a long time. I choose not to because I honestly can't afford to. I easily put on weight and have always felt bigger and fatter than what people think of me. I know this is probably common with most human beings, but sometimes I just wish I felt good about myself, inside and out. I have a feeling this trip is going to transform me into the person I want to be, the whole package. Also on this trip though, food is a must . . . anything and everything. Daily we burn thousands of calories, so why not McDonalds? When I was in elementary school, my mother and I went to the same school. She was a fifth grade teacher and I attended Robert Lewis Stevenson in Merritt Island fourth through sixth grade. So I got stuck going with my mom to school in the morning, I didn't mind though, because almost every morning we stopped at the McDonalds on the way. I wouldn't just get a sandwich though; I'd get the breakfast platters with the pancakes, sausage, and eggs, or the steak sandwich and lots of hash browns plus top it all off with a nice large Coke.

Needless to say, I gained a lot of weight in sixth grade and was depressed. I feel horrible for my parents, looking back to the time period of my life.

After leaving breakfast, we started westward on Hwy 100. It was a really nice road, recently repaved and excellent wide shoulders. The hills were alive at last. You could say I was really excited! I'd had enough of straight roads. Coming from training around the Space Coast in Central Florida, my dad wasn't as prepared as I was. I attended Western Carolina University in the Valley of Cullowhee also called the 'Whee', North Carolina. The Appalachian Mountains and the Blue Ridge Parkway are right near the 'Whee'. I'd say for being there for just two years, I learned a lot about mountains.

I am rather tired again today. If my dad really thinks those were hills we rode through, then he is going to be struggling but trucking along on his hybrid Raleigh. He calls it, "The 'Beast". The 'hills' around Melrose, Florida kicked my dad's butt. At one point, I was easily a few miles ahead when I finally got stopped by a construction worker. I'd say confidently that if he hadn't stopped me I would have been way too far ahead. It took my dad over ten minutes to appear in sight over the last hill. The largest hill was like two hundred and twenty feet.

We followed the ACA route to the Gainesville-Hawthorne State Bike Trail. Fifteen miles of fun, shady canopies, and a large pathway was a nice change from the past days of constant sun beating down on us. Right away we met this cyclist training for an upcoming century ride, and he told us about the area. I am going to refer to him as Jesus because of the way he guided us through the trail. He wasn't carrying equipment and was working on speed, so right away he saw how slow we were going and said he'd catch up with us later. He was our first cyclist that we ran into while riding — totally neat! Along the way, Dad and I just joked about nothing and took a few pictures. This is really fun. I love riding my bicycle! We came up to a middle school, and the schoolyard fence backed up to the trail. Three young girls were hanging from the chain link fence, knuckles wrapped around tightly, as they shook the fence to get our attention. It was a bizarre sight, almost like a prison yard. What they said next though, you would never guess. One squeaky voice shouted to us, "You want to buy some heroine?!!" I couldn't help but bust out laughing. I laughed for maybe twenty minutes after. Too funny. Like who do they think they are? My dad actually told one girl that he was already "high". I didn't know if that was something he should have said, but it sure confused them. When she asked what he was on, he said simply, "Riding my bike." Out of the blue, Jesus appeared again. He guided us to the original springs for Gainesville. This was a neat find, since it had a public bathroom and an amazing ice-cold water fountain!

Eventually, we made it to Gainesville where I am now writing this entry from a room at a Holiday Inn. It happens to be right across the street from the front of the University of Florida. Riding down University Way, I got really annoyed though. Dumb-acting girls were simply not paying attention to any of their surroundings, not even lights or cars. More than a handful of girls had their noses in their phones, texting and walking. Kind of looked like zombies if you ask me. I actually yelled at a few to move, because I had no room to go around them on the sidewalks. Right away we got our normal routine done and were feeling hungry when we noticed that we hadn't eaten since 9:00 A.M. this morning. That is not good! We ended up just going to the downstairs restaurant to chow down at the bar. I sufficiently stuffed myself full. I took my dad on a tour of UF, and that was fun, especially on a 'Thirsty Thursday!' Makes me think back to just last year and my college life; now that was wild. Who would have thought I would be here where I am right now!

"So where is the school?" Mike

"Across the street." Jocelyn

Bridges: 15, Road Kill: 4, Run Offs: 3

Headed west in North Florida

Riding the Gainesville-Hawthorne State Bike Trail

Day 4: Farms, Churches, and Cemeteries
Friday, September 9th, 2011; 66 miles –
Total so Far: 264 miles

We had enjoyed a nice evening in Gator Town, so we slept in until 7:00 A.M. Packing and loading still took over an hour, but we were getting better. We knew where most of the stuff was. I think the trick is not to remove the panniers unless necessary. We walked to the Red Mango across from UF and enjoyed a nice breakfast smoothie. We then checked out and noticed a bike shop across the street. I thought it would be cool to visit our first bike shop, so we walked the bikes in to top off the tire pressure. The shop guy wasn't impressed with all our stuff as I asked him for some air.

"Outside," he said.

Now I had to gingerly back The Beast up without hitting any of the display bikes. Jocelyn pointed out the air hose on the outside wall and said, "Didn't you see it, Dad?" So much for making an impression with a bike shop. Getting out of Gainesville was a real chore, like Daytona, as it was rush hour. And it was very hilly. We stopped at Devil's Millhopper Geological State Park to use the facilities and look around. The park was laid out in a forest of pine trees.

As we continued west, we found ourselves in mile after mile of rolling farmland. The fresh air and speed runs were fun. There were lots of horse farms, along with a wide assortment of other animals. There was church after church, sometimes right next door to each other, and they all seemed to have an attached cemetery. It is really beautiful country up there. During the hill work of the day before, it was mostly a knee-jerk reaction to the shifting just to get over the hills. Today, I really thought about what I was doing and started to correctly time my shifting. I still didn't like all the noise my bike was making, but I just shrugged it off. Of course Jocelyn rode smoothly with little shifting.

We stopped for lunch in High Springs at a small renovated old house after asking directions at the local bike shop for a good lunch spot. The proprietor of this bike shop showed real interest in our adventure. He had a cute dog that took real interest in Jocelyn. During the entire trip, dogs seemed to be attracted to her. She was really missing her dog Yaki at home. For lunch we each had a delicious sandwich and then stopped by the bike shop again for more directions. We were scheduled to meet Andee and Cary along with Jocelyn's friend Matty in Perry the next day. He told us it was another 70 miles to Perry but there were a few small towns and campgrounds along the way.

The miles ticked away as we enjoyed the many farms. I have never seen such a variety of cows. We were also chased by lots and lots of dogs. It is sort of nerve-racking as you come along a house on the side of the road with a fence and a yard full of dogs barking and running. You are certainly glad the fence is there until at the end of the property, when the fence suddenly ends! House after house was like this — the fence ends and all hell breaks loose. We had some close calls but didn't quite get bitten. Jocelyn took the brunt of this as she was riding in the rear. There was one time when I quickly rang my bike bell and the dog left Jocelyn and came after me! This went on and on for miles. Even dogs on the other side of the road chased us. We were afraid of them getting run over, but they were pretty smart and would stop when a car approached. It turned out to be a good way to work off our lunch.

Around dusk we spotted a sign for the Suwannee River Rendezvous Resort and Campground outside the town of Mayo. We rode two miles down a dirt road and came upon a cool-looking resort. There were cabins, tent and RV sites, and a lodge. We chose the lodge, as the mosquitoes were already coming out and we were more than ready for some air conditioning. We quickly settled into our tiny room, did the laundry, and then went to the main lodge building for dinner. We enjoyed a delicious hamburger along with a few beers. It was karaoke night and Jocelyn was thinking about joining in, but she decided not to. She was missing her karaoke partner Matty. For dessert we split a delicious hot fudge sundae. As we walked back to our room, I was already thinking about breakfast. Long bike rides burn the calories, so you can eat whatever you want. It was another good day and a good night.

Jocelyn: We slept in till 7:00 A.M. We're both still trying to get a hold of unloading and loading and packing efficiently. It blows my mind that we're living with such little supplies of things. Makes me really think about why I have so many things at home. I guess you could call me a collector. Ever since middle school, I got into style more too. That's probably because the three years prior I was at an elementary school that had a uniform. And then before that my mom basically dressed me. She still helps me pick out clothing and such. I have an eccentric taste; that's for sure. On our bicycles we have front and back panniers. My back panniers hold clothing and other random miscellaneous things.

After having a good smoothie at Red Mango, we hit up a local bike shop to top off my dad's tires. My tubes have Presta valves that need a Schrader adaptor for use on public pumps, but we hadn't found our adaptor yet. Getting out of Gainesville during rush hour wasn't that much fun. We soon found ourselves in some rolling farmland. I loved lifting my head while I was in my down bars position to breathe in the fresh air. Not to mention racing my dad down the hills was fun too! This part didn't remind me of Florida at all, maybe South Carolina, but in fact, we were still in Florida. It is only the fourth day. I feel like we could be farther if we didn't follow the ACA route. It kind of took us a weird way across Florida, like straight north up the coast and than west but then southwest to Gainesville. I feel like we could have just kept west completely, but maybe we're avoiding more hills, which my dad is happy about I'm sure. Today, I give props to my dad. He really started to get a handle of shifting and timing it just right when gearing down and up. So I am sure he will get the hang of it soon enough.

For lunch we rode into High Springs and talked to a bicycle shop owner about lunch options. It seemed to have one main street where little ma and pa shops resided, a neat little springs town. We ate at a small renovated old house café and had homemade grilled cheese and tuna salad sandwiches. So delicious! Once back on the road, the day became very stressful. Not knowing where exactly we might end up was very nerve racking. We're in fact going to have many days like this. That's mainly because both of us decided that on this trip we were going to just take the ride as one big adventure and not planning out ending points at all. Typical cross-country cyclists plan everything out, from start to finish, assuring they have rest areas with food options and etc., but we're adventure seekers. This could cause some problems though.

There seemed to be many angry drivers on the road today. I think I counted nine cars that honked at us in a time period of two hours. I guess I can't really say if it was because they were upset at us for riding in the bike lane on the shoulder of the road or they we're supporting us and giving us a positive honk to keep going sort of thing. Who knows? I do know the ones that yelled out their window were mostly being rude. I don't understand that. Honestly, I can't hear you if you decide to scream something at me. So it's rather a waste of someone's breath to be mean like that. I am a really nice person, and I believe you should treat everyone as you wish to be treated. I respect you; you respect me. But when some random dude sticks his head out to yell at us for biking on the road, I am of course going to throw him the middle finger. My dad didn't see that though.

We must have rode for hours on US 27, along numerous farm fields. Our first encounter with dogs was frightening. The first time my dad was riding in front and this dog bolted straight off his property and straight for my bike. Definitely scary to see all the dogs' teeth and to hear their loud growling and barking. I actually unclipped in case the dog decided to try and make my leg a meal. I cannot imagine kicking a dog, but if it comes to making sure my leg is well enough to ride, than I feel as though it has to happen. It is funny when you see a dog on the other side of a fence running after you because they can't actually get through the fence, until the fence ends, but then it's not funny.

Lucking out, we rode right by an open campground. Just two miles north of US 27 on the Suwannee River, we found a neat place. Suwannee River Rendezvous Resort and Campground is beautiful and in the process of being a renovated resort with a woodsy lodge feel. The sunset bounced through the trees and onto the Suwannee River which was running at a slow one mph flow. I studied the map at dinner, and the Suwannee has so many springs tucked in along it. Both Dad and I have decided that we want to come back with family and friends. Canoeing, snorkeling, and fishing are very appealing! The kitchen and lodge was a nice place to relax and chow down. Grandma Susie's Cookin' Shack had some real good comfort food. We already have an idea what we want for breakfast. After listening to karaoke and groups of families playing twenty questions trivia, we had an entertaining time. I found out that my dad didn't enjoy playing games like that, and neither did I. I probably picked that up from him because I know my mom enjoys games. She is a schoolteacher, after all.

Day 5: A Short Ride to Perry
Saturday, September 10, 2011; 35 miles –
Total so Far: 299 miles

We slept in until the sun woke us at 7:30 A.M. The lodge is surrounded by trees, so very little light entered the room. We walked down to the kitchen and had a delicious homemade breakfast with everything, including the pancakes from scratch. There were no mixes here. After breakfast, Jocelyn wrote in her journal and I hiked around the grounds. I talked with the owner as he was loading up several canoes to take them upriver. Lots of people come and ride the canoes down the Suwannee River to this resort, and it looks like a lot of fun. We would like to return here with our canoe and rent a cabin. It is definitely a fun location.

The ride to Perry was uneventful except for the occasional dog getting through the fences. Then we came upon several chicken farms. The smell got us before we saw them. There would be row upon row of huge chicken houses. We also rode by a huge prison outside the town of Mayo. We decided it must be a high-security prison, because the coiled razor wire covered the entire fence and not just the top.

A few miles outside of Perry, we heard a car approaching with the horn blaring. I thought, *Great! Our first encounter with an angry motorist.* We hadn't had any problems yet, but it was Andee and Cary! They pulled over ahead of us, and Cary brought us each out an ice-cold beer! We drank them right on the roadside. It was so refreshing on such a hot day.

After a few beers, Andee and Cary continued to a Holiday Inn in Perry where she had booked two rooms. We soon arrived, along with Jocelyn's friend Matty from Florida State University (FSU). We unloaded everything again but this time took several items and gave them to Andee to take home. "We don't need this stuff," we explained. Jocelyn also suggested that I transfer more weight to her panniers to ease my load. What a nice daughter! We found a really good and popular fish house for dinner. Afterwards, Jocelyn provided some entertainment by showing the patrons her Dub Step dancing, and she received a roaring round of applause.

That night I talked with my sister Tish. My dad had gone into the hospital and was not doing well. I was able to talk with him, and he was very pleased that Jocelyn and I were on our bikes. He was in and out on medication, but I heard him say, "Keep those wheels going round and round." At that point, I was crying on the phone with my sister and trying to figure out what to do. I said, "I'm going to continue the ride." I felt really bad and continued to anguish over what to do. We had been planning to take the next day off, as Cary wanted to show us some good snorkeling areas in the nearby gulf, but I decided that I needed to ride to clear my head. I was very disappointed for Cary, and I knew Jocelyn wanted a break and to visit more with Matty. That night I hardly slept as I thought about my dad in the hospital. The doctors still had some more tests to run, but he didn't want to be touched anymore. We had said our goodbyes. He wanted me to continue.

(As I write this on March 24th, 2012, from Antarctica, tears come to my eyes. My dad would have been 90 years old today. Happy Birthday, Dad!)

Jocelyn: This morning was by far the most peaceful of mornings. We had a nice huge breakfast, cooked to order, outside on a picnic table and watched the day begin with the animals rising from their sleep and the water flowing continuously faster. It was a short ride today. In the beginning, I was practically calling it our "rest" day, but that judgment quickly changed. It turned into one of the worst days in the fact that it was over 100 degrees F, and at the end of just mile five I found myself already watching the distance like a hawk, therefore making the thirty-five mile ride feel like a seventy mile ride. It also didn't help that I was super excited to see my mother, my brother, and my brain twin, Matty, in Perry, Florida. They're meeting us for the weekend. Stoked because I haven't seen them in five days and I missed them. Matty is driving up from Tallahassee. She goes to Florida State University and we have known each other since first grade! Our friendship means the world to me, so I was excited to be reunited.

We'd been riding west on US 27 and literally saw just a handful of cars. Just a few miles out of Perry, we heard a car approaching with the horn honking. Both my dad and I turned around and were thrilled to see that it was my mother and brother! After pulling over, my brother jumps out with an ice-cold beer for my dad, and my dad gave me the honorable first sip. I felt the cold, icy beer touch my sun-dried lips and slide down my parched throat, and in an instant I was refreshed. Beer is refreshing. I gave it back to my dad. I was pleasantly pleased from just that sip. We both drank a beer just on the side of the road and talked to our family. It was nice, and after deciding what hotel we wanted to check out, they quickly went ahead of us to book two rooms. Riding into Perry was nice with my dad; we both were talking about how refreshing that beer was and how we couldn't wait to have another one!

Once we reached the hotel, our reality sank in. The lifestyle we'd been living the past five days had already changed us some. At least I'd say that because I found myself irritated with my mother being in the way of our routine. After getting a room, we unloaded only the valuables we needed off the bike, which were clothes, toiletries, sandals, and other miscellaneous things. After we got cleaned up and washed clothes, Matty finally arrived! We went to a local favorite seafood restaurant that didn't serve beer, so my dad was a little upset. In the middle of the meal, out of nowhere, "Cotton Eyed Joe" blasted through speakers, and this lady began to dance around the tables with an unfamiliar instrument. It's called a "Pogo Stick" and it was used to attract giant earthworms to the surface. How wild is that? I enjoyed watching her dance with it. Reminded me of the style dancing I enjoy, dub step, trance style moves when I dance. Being on stage for dancing was sort of a first for me, but I enjoyed it, and I could tell that this lady enjoyed her pogo stick dancing. I actually got asked to dance with her after our meal because my very social mother told her about my style. So everyone turned to watch as I danced to her playing the pogo stick. It was fun! I was nervous at first but than just let loose. I still can't believe I danced dub step to "Cotton Eyed Joe". That means it's a very versatile form of dance.

Today was an overall good day, minus the ride, but everything else was fun. I am so excited to wake up tomorrow and know that I don't have to get back on the saddle. Finally — a rest day.

Day 6: A Long Hot Ride
Sunday, September 11, 2011; 67 miles –
Total so Far: 366 miles

I was up early. Andee was very worried about me, as I asked her to wake up the kids and let them know we were getting back on the road already. They weren't too pleased, but I needed to think. There is no greater place to think than on a bicycle saddle, letting the miles roll by. We had the buffet breakfast at the hotel, walked the bikes out, and said our goodbyes. Andee and Cary followed us for a few miles, beeped the horn, and were gone after this very short visit. We did what we do best: we pedaled away the miles on Hwy 98.

The scenery was beautiful as we passed over several small bridges with clear, blue-green water underneath. It was a very hot day with Jocelyn's bike thermometer reading in the low 100s. The water continued to flow through us, and we were almost empty already when the small town of Newport appeared. On the right was Ouzts Too Oyster Bar and Grill. The sign read, "Bikers Welcome" so we stopped but it was full of motorcycle bikers, which was fine. As often happens when we travel into these small towns, you never know about the food situation. Sometimes there are only quick food marts, and other times just one restaurant. I'm glad we stopped here as it was the only place in town. We split the blackened grouper sandwich which was excellent along with two cold draft beers. I was feeling sorry for Jocelyn as she enjoys beer like I do but she isn't 21 yet. That milestone would occur somewhere on the road — probably Texas.

I was carrying along an iPod Nano but hadn't really used it yet. The road was good here and quiet so I put on the ear buds. Between the two beers and

Bob Dylan, we quickly came to a campground that looked inviting. As we entered, the manager was leaving but said to just pitch our tent anywhere and she would square up with us in the morning. The only campers were RVs, but we found a nice, empty spot right on a bay. Our first camp, and we were excited as we set up our tent for the first time. We had also bought the Hubba-Hubba Gear Shed that connects on one side. This provided a waterproof enclosure for all our panniers and stuff. It worked out well. We did not put the tent fly on as it looked like it wasn't going to rain. This gave us some real outdoor living as we would simply sleep in a screened enclosure. We locked the bikes together around a large tree with the two 10 foot cable locks. What a great idea, and it worked well throughout the trip. We had also purchased two Arkle rainproof covers large enough to fit around a fully-loaded bike without removing the panniers. Once again, these covers are great as everything under them stays dry.

We did the laundry and hung it out on our clothesline. We were proud of ourselves and decided to cross the street to a beachside restaurant for dinner. This restaurant turned out to be a pretty-fancy place. We were totally underdressed but didn't care. We sat outside on the balcony and enjoyed the beautiful bayside view. I ate the local scallops while Jocelyn had pasta. On the way back to camp we bought a 4-pack of beer. Throughout the first half of the trip, 4-packs became the norm as 6-packs were not available.

Back at the camp, I had a nice conversation with a man in a neighboring RV. He was fascinated by our trip and said he wished he had as good a relationship with his daughter as I had with Jocelyn. When we left the next day, he came up to me, gave me a $20 bill, and said to enjoy lunch on him.

The sunset was absolutely beautiful and we took several pictures. I called my sister and learned that my dad was worse. He wasn't cognizant anymore. Tish held the phone to his ear and I talked to him, but there was no response. I told him that I loved him. Tish told me he did move and might have recognized my voice. Jocelyn and I went to sleep. How bad can a guy feel?

Jocelyn: We decided to skip our day off today and ride to the Gulf Coast. We had a nice relaxing but short time with my family and Matty yesterday afternoon and night. Please keep my Grandpa, my dad's father, in your thoughts and prayers. A rough ride ahead, but we will keep riding, Grandpa. We're coming. I love you.

Our family as we ride out of Perry, Florida

A Gulf Coast campsite

Day 7: Another Hot but Pretty Ride
Monday, September 12, 2011; 69 miles –
Total so Far: 435 miles

We woke to a beautiful sunrise and spent two hours breaking camp and loading the bikes. This was so much work, but with us working as a team we did fine! On our way out, the manager was at the office so I stopped to pay. When I asked how much, she said the total was $37!

"What?" We had just pitched a tent and did not use any hookups!

"$37," she repeated. It did not matter that we were not an RV, as all campers pay the same. I was shocked but handed over the credit card. What else was I to do?

We continued riding west on Hwy 98 and the temperature was another scorcher. We were now riding directly on the coast and the butterflies were plentiful. They were all over the road and on us too! It was still in the 100s. We passed a sign that read, 'Welcome to Tate's Hell State Forest'. It was hot but we didn't bother to check out 'Tate's Hell'. We rode several miles to the town of Carrabelle where we stopped for lunch at an old-time fountain diner called Carrabelle Junction. It was another excellent stop where it seemed all the locals hung out. We were glad we spotted this gem, as there were several other chain establishments available. We enjoyed another great lunch and even had malted milk for dessert. I paid with the $20 that last night's neighbor had given us.

We were completely fueled to continue for many more miles and soon found ourselves in Apalachicola after crossing several large bridges. It was a fun ride, and we continued to Port St. Joe and to an old converted building called Port Inn. As I checked in, I asked the clerk about local storage facilities and transportation to Panama City International Airport. Not knowing what to do was really affecting Jocelyn and me. As I searched the Internet for flights, Jocelyn finally said, "Dad, we need to go to see Grandpa."

She was right and it was time for some action.

Jocelyn: After a long and rough 70 mile day, we decided to stop in Port St. Joe. My dad's father hasn't much time, so our trip is on hold. When we return, we will start back here in St. Joe. We've ridden a total of 435 miles thus far. Now our focus will be turned to our family and flying to California — somehow.

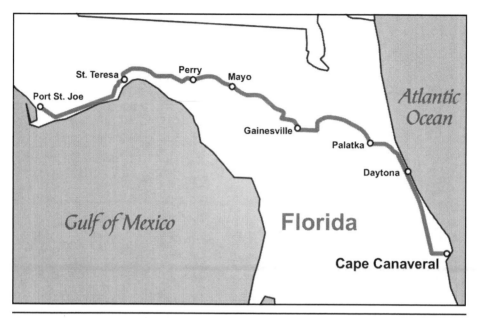

Day 1-Day 7: Cape Canaveral, Florida to Port St. Joe, Florida

Chapter 3:
Our Mission is on Hold

Day 8: Our Adventure Will Be
on Hold for Two Weeks
Tuesday September 13, 2011; 0 miles -
Total so Far: 435 miles

I was up most of the night wondering if we should ride into Panama City, store the bikes, go to the airport, or to just leave from here. My Internet searching really didn't get anywhere. It appeared as though we would spend a few thousand dollars for ticketing as my Delta miles were not being accepted. I called Delta and got the same runaround. The bottom line was that we didn't need to spend more hours on the bike because we needed to get home to my dad in Oxnard, California. There was a storage facility in Port St. Joe and a taxi ride was around $100. We ate breakfast at the Inn, and then I called the storage facility. It was only a mile inland, so we were soon there and rented a small storage unit that would just fit both bikes side by side.

While we were unloading some clothes and a pannier for each of us to take, one of the workers, Charles, stopped by and asked about our bike trip. He seemed very interested, and when we told him about our plight he wanted to help. He was leaving soon to take a load of scrap to Panama City and offered to take us to the airport. We were more than happy to say yes. By the time we each had a pannier ready to go, he pulled up with his truck and trailer and we were off.

Over an hour later he dropped us off curbside. I gave him some money for gas and his time. Charles also gave me his phone number and said to call him when we get back and he would pick us up. I have read a lot of bike journals, and one thing that really stands out is the kindness of people you meet along the way. So far we had only traveled seven days but had met so many nice and helpful people.

We walked up to the Delta ticket counter and explained our situation. The agent did some searching on his computer but didn't come up with much and wasn't able to use our miles. He directed us to the airport business center computers and gave us a number to call. So Jocelyn and I worked together on their computer and phone to have my frequent flyer miles cover both our flights. We then returned to the same agent and said that our miles now worked. He did some more searching and got us upgrades and earlier flights. The next flight to Atlanta was leaving soon. He gave us our boarding passes, and since we didn't have anything to check in, he said, "Run." We did and we made the flight and also the connection from Atlanta to Los Angeles.

We were met by my brother-in-law Jim around 11:00 P.M. When we got to his truck, he turned around and said, "I'm sorry to have to tell you this, but your dad passed away two hours ago."

We drove up to Oxnard where my sister Tish was waiting. I felt bad that we hadn't left just a day earlier, but she said Dad wasn't coherent for the last 24 hours. I didn't think that we would see Andee and Cary so soon after Perry. The next two weeks were a blur. My mom had passed away three years earlier and we repeated everything for my dad. We saw lots of family and friends who had been following our ride. Most of them wondered what we were going to do now. I told everyone what my dad had told me the last time I'd talked with him: "Keep those wheels going round and round and I will be with you all the way."

Exactly two weeks later, we returned to Panama City International Airport, and true to his word, Charles and his wife were waiting for us.

Chapter 4:
"Keep the Wheels Going Round and Round"

Day 9: A Ride for My Dad and Jocelyn's Grandpa... On the Road Again
Tuesday September 27, 2011; 1 mile – Total so far 436 miles

Charles dropped us off at the storage shed and we checked out. The bikes were waiting for us but Jocelyn's rear tire had a flat. I changed out the tube and refilled all our tires at the rental shop. It was close to 4:00 P.M., and since we had been up pretty much all night and day with our red-eye flight, it was an easy decision to return to the Port Inn for another night. We rode the one mile back and stayed in our same one-bedroom suite. After repacking again and doing some laundry — in a washing machine and dryer — we walked through the old, little town of Port St. Joe. We found a nice Italian restaurant called Joe Mama's Wood Fired Pizza and settled on an excellent pizza and two glasses of a fine red wine. After dinner, we walked to the gulf and took several pictures of the beautiful sunset. What a beautiful gulf-side town! We then retired to our room for an early bedtime.

It was time to get back in the saddle and we were two weeks down. We still wanted to be at Tish and Jim's house for Thanksgiving, but were not going to push it. We decided that this adventure should not be rushed. We had a new outlook on the ride and were very eager to get back on the road again.

Jocelyn: Tomorrow my dad and I will be back on the road, back to the living in the day to day moment within the bicycle lanes. Even though our journey has never ended, now we take with us the adventures we had in California for the past two weeks. I will cherish my Grandpa's spirit along the trails and hear him say, "Just keep peddling." I look forward to keep riding on this journey of a lifetime! I know now the first challenge I will face and have been facing, and that is motivation to keep moving forward and to not look at the final destination but to look at each day and the journey within it.

Day 10: A Good Start, Lousy Middle, and Nice Ending
Wednesday September 28, 2011; 73 miles – Total so far: 509 miles

We finally left the Port Inn for good after a full breakfast. It was great to be on the road again. We flew through Mexico Beach with its beautifully-groomed white-sand beaches and watched several jets fly over us as we rode past Tyndal A.F.B. The fun ended when the shoulder stopped on the bridge over St. Andrews Bay. We would not see a shoulder again for over 10 miles. We negotiated the road and sidewalk, which were full of cars and people. The sidewalks all had telephone poles in the middle with an occasional sign mounted on two posts. It was an obstacle course. This was where I almost got hit by a van. Jocelyn was looking out for me and yelled out as a van turned right in front of me. I had established eye contact with the driver and he saw me going straight through an intersection, but he did not want to stop. I hit the brakes and he continued. I reminded myself that I must pay more attention!

We continued and finally saw where all the logging trucks were headed — to the huge Springfield Paper Mill. Since we were in Springfield, we thought of Homer Simpson, as he might work here! The weather grew worse with lightening and rain as we continued through Panama City. We took shelter in a bike shop and were given directions on how to stay out of the worst of the traffic. We also ducked into a few churches to get out of the lightening. Rain poured down as we rode across the bridge to Panama City Beach. Once the lightening dissipated, we continued along, decked out in all our rain gear. We rode beachside and stopped at the Lotus Café where we scored a great lunch. Jocelyn's Thai food was so hot she was offered gloves while she ate so she wouldn't burn her fingers. I wondered, *What does that do to your insides?!*

Panama City Beach was full of bikers on motorcycles participating in the local bike week called Thunder Beach. We stopped for several pictures as we rode through Laguna Beach and Santa Monica. Just by looking at the signs, I would think we were in California! But these were Southeastern towns. We came upon a huge resort area and checked at two state parks for camping, but there was no camping at these parks even though one was named Camp Helen State Park.

Dusk approached as we stopped at Grayton State Park. We checked in as the ranger station was closing and then pedaled another mile to a food mart for some beer and sandwiches. By the time we got to our campsite, it was dark. It was no fun setting up a campsite in the dark, especially when I couldn't find my headband light!

As we were finishing up with the tent (no laundry tonight!), a fellow biker rode by looking for a place to pitch his tent. "Plenty of space here," I said. Dominic told us that he was from England and was touring the U.S. for three months. After he had his tent pitched, I offered him an ice-cold beer. My beach cooler sure came in handy. He even laughed when I showed it to him. He couldn't believe I carried that on my bike. "I don't," I said. "Jocelyn carries it and sometimes with beer!" We enjoyed sitting up late and swapping bike stories. Fun times indeed. It was time for some much-needed sleep, but the local critters had other plans.

Jocelyn: We have made it to Grayton, Fl. We rode 73 miles in some of the worst conditions yet. Road was horrible at times with no shoulders and the sidewalks were worse. Rain poured down on us for a solid 4 hrs. Still soaked and about to camp out! Met a guy now who is camping with us and has ridden from Chicago. Pretty awesome. Good night friends. No electric tonight.

Admiring beautiful Mexico Beach

Day 11: A Stressful Ride but Lots of Good Honks
Thursday September 29, 2011; 45 miles –
Total so Far: 554

We went to sleep with the tent fly off. The stars were plentiful once again. In the middle of the night I was awakened by rustling noises around the camp. I couldn't see anything so I grabbed my flashlight. When I turned it on, there was a raccoon walking right by the tent. Since there was only a thin screen separating us from the outside, it was a little unnerving. As I moved the light around, I saw several critters scavenging around. I left the tent and checked out all our stuff on the picnic table. They had found our dinner leftovers! After I cleaned up, I noticed how wet everything was and thought it might rain, so I attached the fly and crawled back in. As I lay there sweating, I thought, *This isn't comfortable!* so I exited again and removed the fly and went back to sleep. I didn't sleep much while hearing all the critters walking around. I was happy when daylight came. I guess I wasn't that good of a camper yet!

Of course Jocelyn and Dominic had slept through it all. One of the raccoons had dug into my Camelback water backpack, removed a banana, actually peeled it, ate the banana, and left the peel! I walked around a bit now that there was light. It was a beautiful, wooded campground with the beach beyond a small pond. About 30 feet from our tent was a sign that read: "ALLIGATORS - SWIM WITH CAUTION!"

We were up at 6:30 A.M. but didn't ride away until 9:30. The tent and everything else was wet from very heavy dew. We packed everything, knowing that we would have to dry it out at the first opportunity. As we said our goodbyes to Dominic, we noticed that he was riding a Surly Long Haul Trucker just like Jocelyn.

We were finally on the road and looked for breakfast in Santa Rosa Beach, but there was nothing around. So we headed back up to Hwy 98 where we finally found a restaurant and had a delicious brunch. After that, it was a stressful ride negotiating the roads and sidewalks of Destin, Fort Walton Beach, and beyond. We generally do not like riding on sidewalks but are sometimes forced to do so because of traffic. This was one of those days. The shoulders came and went. There seemed to be no planning for bicycle traffic along this stretch. It got so bad that I called for a timeout after having to walk up a bridge without any shoulder. I was disrupted while climbing the bridge and couldn't get my bike going again as it would not shift correctly. This was my first premonition of bike problems. After our timeout, we realized we would probably not get to Pensacola that day.

We rode into Navarre Beach and stopped at the first motel. We were very disappointed by our 45 miles but figured we couldn't get to Pensacola until after 8:00 P.M., so that was it for the day. Since all our camping gear was stowed away wet, we pulled it all out and it quickly dried in the setting sun. There was a laundry room on the premises, so we did two days' worth, the lazy way, with lots of quarters. Then we went next door and pigged out on the KFC chicken bowls. There must be 1000 calories in those bowls filled with mashed potatoes, chicken, and gravy, but we knew we would work that off the next day. We slept well thinking we should finally get out of Florida tomorrow. It would be a long day of riding, but unknown to us, we were going to be tested once again.

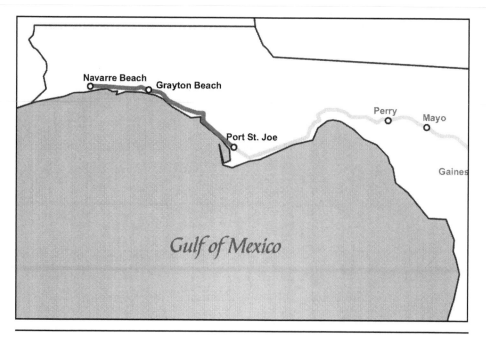

Day 9-Day 11: Port St. Joe, Florida to Navarre Beach, Florida

Chapter 5:
Close to an Abort

Day 12: A Nice Sandy Beach ride,
a Hard Fall, and Another Delay
Friday September 30, 2011; 18 miles -
Total so Far: 572 miles

The morning brought a beautiful day with a fresh headwind as we traveled along a sandy road through Navarre Beach and into Santa Rosa Island. We felt as if we were riding on the beach. There was no traffic, and Jocelyn chatted with friends on her cell phone. I just admired the peaceful view. We took turns taking pictures of each other and both together while riding. We saw several gigantic condos about a mile off and knew that this beautiful ride would soon be over — and it certainly was. The fall happened very quickly and without warning.

Suddenly I was in the ambulance, watching Jocelyn disappear as we drove past her. The paramedics knew I was upset and tried to comfort me by asking questions about our trip. Soon we arrived at Gulf Breeze Hospital. This was my first ride in an ambulance. I was taken to a room, and it was a huge relief to see the fire/rescue guys walk in with my bike. Nice guys! I was immediately taken to X-ray, and the nurse practitioner confirmed a completely broken #11 rib. "That's one of the worst you can break since it is a floating rib," she said.

"Of course it is," I replied. I was having a really hard time breathing and talking, so the nurse gave me a morphine injection that quickly calmed me down. In the meantime, Jocelyn had walked in with her bike. They weren't going to let her bring the bike in but she did anyway. That's Jocelyn. I looked around and didn't see my helmet and backpack. I asked the nurse if she could get hold of the guys that brought my bike in and see if my helmet and pack were still in their truck. She did, and they came in about ten minutes later. It seemed like I was more worried about my bike and stuff than about myself. But when you are on a trip like this, all that stuff is your life right now. I was determined more than ever to keep the adventure going.

The bottom line was that I needed to rest at least a week before getting back on my bike. But first we needed a place to stay. The nurse was amazing, as she recommended a nice motel on the bay and offered her son to load up both bikes and take us there. Wow! Everyone in Gulf Breeze Hospital was so nice and did more than their job. Her son arrived shortly, and with the morphine doing its work, I was able to walk out, get in his truck, and ride to the motel to check in. We were able to get a nice big room right on the water. *Not bad for convalescing*, I thought. We then walked to the local drug store for prescription meds and some beer. We walked back to the room where I self-medicated with the beer, and then we ate. That's all I remember of that day!

Jocelyn: My dad was caught by a huge gust of wind that pushed him into heavy sand. He fell really hard, and I had no time to brake. My front tire slammed into his ribs, and I went flying over. He has a lot of bad cuts that I bandaged up, but he had sharp pain and bruising on his left side. I'm shaken up and don't know if he will be okay. It's my fault; I should have cut into the sand.

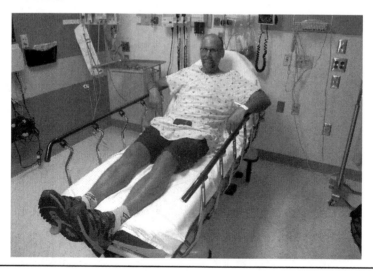

The emergency room at Gulf Breeze Hospital. Why was I smiling with a broken rib?

Day 13: We are Ready for Another Start Tomorrow
Thursday October 6th, 2011; 0 miles –
Total so Far: 572

I have been recuperating in a nice bayside motel room in the town of Gulf Breeze, which is a long bridge ride away from Pensacola. I had a very rude awakening that first morning in the motel as I could not get out of bed due to immense pain. Whenever I moved, my left side would go into a deep spasm. I was stuck. I yelled for Jocelyn to help me, and she managed to get me out of the bed. From there it just went downhill. "This is not good," I said. Between phone calls the night before and this morning, we tried to figure out the best thing to do. Andee wanted Cary to drive my truck up, load the bikes, and take us home. Then, when I was well enough to ride, Cary would bring us back here. This was out of the question, as I did not want to go home. That would be negative miles in my book, and I only wanted to go west.

Another option would be to have Jocelyn's friend Matty from FSU come and pick us up and take us back to Tallahassee (about 200 miles), where I could convalesce. That seemed like a good plan because we were also in touch with a neighbor's relative in town who offered to store our bikes and gear. Matty arrived on the second day, and we went out to eat. I needed a lot of help getting in and out of Matty's car. After dinner, I decided that because of my very limited mobility, I would stay in Gulf Breeze. I just didn't need to be moving around. That night, Jocelyn returned with Matty to Tallahassee and I relegated myself to sleeping in the chair. At least in the chair I had the side arms to push up with.

Jocelyn: As a result of my father's broken rib, we are stuck in Pensacola, Florida for now. So close to Alabama! He is recovering in the hotel room, and I am with friends in Tallahassee. Because of the amount of pain he is in, he did not want me seeing it anymore. He saw how much it was upsetting me because I actually did this to him. This freak accident might put us on another setback. We both just want to get moving and get to riding.

Mike: The next morning brought very little pain relief. The nurse had given me a tube with a ball to breathe into. This was to keep my lungs exercised to prevent pneumonia. I took a short walk and worked on my lung capacity. I also went to the front desk and asked for a discount, since we now needed the room for a week. Each day I walked more and breathed harder. My side was still very painful, but I wasn't going to give up. I probably pushed myself too much, but that's the way I am. By Wednesday I wanted no more of the meds, because I needed to have a clear head for our planned restart on Friday. The big test came when I wheeled my bike without the panniers out the door. It was only Wednesday, but I needed to know if I could even get on The Beast. I did and almost fell off from the pain. But I rode in the local neighborhood for a mile or so before I had to get off, and I barely did without falling again. *This restart is going to be the hardest thing I have ever done,* I thought.

Cary drove up to Tallahassee, picked up Jocelyn, and then drove to Gulf Breeze. We had a fun afternoon driving to the beach where I had fallen and then went to downtown Pensacola for an excellent fish dinner at the Fish House Restaurant. I was doing better; at least I could get in and out of the car. It would be nice to sleep in a bed, but for now I had graduated up to a chaise lounge I had brought into the room from the pool. On Thursday morning, Cary and Jocelyn rented two Stand Up Paddle (SUP) boards from next door and paddled around the bay for a few hours while I sat and read. I enjoyed the nice little break with my kids, and they really seemed to enjoy themselves. After that and more driving around the area, we ate at a local Mexican restaurant and then said our goodbyes to Cary. I told him, "I don't want to see you again until San Diego!" We had seen him in Perry, and then in California, and now once again.

It was back to just the two of us again. That meant packing up and loading the panniers. "Will that ever stop?" I wondered. We went to the motel restaurant for a small dinner and retired early. The nurse practitioner had told me that continuing on the trip would depend on my pain tolerance. I had a feeling it would be a very long and painful day.

Jocelyn: Looks like tomorrow might be the day!!! Well, it's been a whole month on this journey, and I don't know what is to come now. I just hope we get to peddling and my dad is actually healthy enough to continue. If not, I don't know what we will do. But for now, I am going to Stand Up Paddle (SUP) out on the Gulf with my brother. Ready to live in the moment and the bike lane once again!

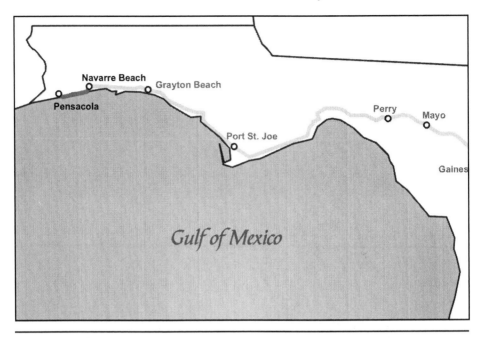

Day 12-Day 13: Navarre Beach, Florida to Pensacola, Florida

Chapter 6:
Resume the Mission

Day 14: Another Slow but Good Restart, and We Finally Make it Out of Florida
Friday October 7, 2011; 67 miles –
Total so Far: 639 miles

As I walked The Beast out the room, I tried to figure out how to get on with all the panniers. After a few false starts, I finally got on the saddle but immediately had to get off because of all the traffic headed into and out of Pensacola. The morning rush hour was on. After standing for several minutes, we saw our chance to move in and made a left turn to enter the Pensacola Bay Bridge. The headwind blew hard as we crossed. I was just trying not to fall, because if I did I would immediately be run over. Near the top of the bridge, a construction crew tried to wrestle down a huge tarp that flapped in the outside lane. I thought that if I could just make it over the bridge we would be fine with an excellent tailwind. We finally crossed the bridge and flew west.

We then traveled through downtown Pensacola and made our way over several more bridges and back to the beach. I was doing okay mostly because we had lucked out with a huge tailwind. In fact, at one point we stopped and took a picture of a flag blowing west. I told Jocelyn that we would not see this very often. Getting on and off the bike was getting easier, because at this point I knew what pain I could tolerate. We soon came to the state line of Alabama and were so excited to finally be out of Florida. For the last two weeks we had heard several comments from people, "Are they STILL in Florida?"

Our first state was complete, and we ventured into Alabama. We still had a great tailwind, so we rode and rode. Our plan was to ferry across Mobile Bay. There were several times we were confused between the ACA map and our GPS. It was a confusing ride, but we did make it to Fort Morgan and the Mobile Bay Ferry. The next ferry left at 2:45, so we bought an ice-cold drink and sat and enjoyed the shady trees. Several people walked up to us and asked about our trip. We never tired of people asking us questions. Before the trip, I had printed up a personal contact card showing both of our bike journal website links. The card was very handy as we talked to people, and we gave a few hundred away along the trip.

We rode our bikes onto the ferry right on time. It was a nice crossing and we saw many natural gas rigs. The ACA map and the GPS showed no lodging for another 50 miles. Since it was almost 4:00 P.M., we asked one of the crew for recommendations on Dauphin Island. He told us there was a campground to the left of the ferry and nothing else. In my condition, I didn't feel like I could lie down in a tent, but there was no other alternative. We arrived at Dauphin Island Campground, but since it was a Friday all the spots were sold out. I explained that we were on bikes with a small tent, and the office clerk managed to find us a spot. We set up camp, showered, and did the laundry before walking into town for dinner. We had been told the town is less than a mile away, but that mile ended up as almost 3 miles!

We were beat by the time we found an open restaurant, and of course they were packed. We sat at the bar and ordered dinner. I wondered how we were going to get back since it was now dark. We struck up conversations with many people, until finally a guy picking up an order to go said he would give us a ride. This guy was a hoot with many stories of his hunting and fishing and working on gas rigs. As we got into his truck he told us, while holding a beer in one hand, to make sure we buckled up as the local police check on that. He drove us back to our camp as he drank his beer! We were beat and retired to our once again fly-less tent. Without too much pain, I lay down and wondered how I was going to get up again. We were soon asleep after staring at a star-filled sky.

Jocelyn: We are in Dauphine Island, Alabama, at a nice campground, but we just had to walk three miles to find an open restaurant. I don't feel like walking back to the tent. I'll be eaten alive — again! We rode a total of 67 miles today. I am so proud of my dad.

Riding on the Mobile Bay Ferry to Dauphin Island

Camping at Dauphin Island Campground

Day 15: A Stressful Day of Riding through Alabama with Little or No Shoulders
Saturday October 8, 2011; 70 miles – Total so Far: 709 miles

Nature called at around 3:00 A.M., and I spent several minutes trying to stand up. I just could not do it, but I didn't want to wake Jocelyn. Since there wasn't any room to roll around, I just popped up and almost screamed. The pain was intense, and I walked it out on the way to the bathroom. When I returned, there was no way I was even going to attempt to lay down again, so I sat on the picnic table and thought, *Now what?* I unpacked my laptop and checked the MiFi for a signal, and to my surprise it connected to 4G! Most of Florida was 3G. I spent a few hours under our camp light updating my journal on the Crazy Guy website. It worked out really well. Jocelyn woke up and got her Facebook updated too. It's always nice to start the day with both of the sites updated.

It only took us one hour to break camp and load due to great teamwork. Our neighbors came over with fresh biscuits, jam, and orange juice. What a treat! We then cycled to the end of Dauphin Island and toured around Fort Gaines, a key fort in the Civil War's Battle of Mobile Bay in 1864. The ocean was extremely rough, with a hard wind blowing from the northeast. We pedaled west to the center of the island with the wind and then turned northeast to cross the enormous Gordon Persons Bridge. An extremely daunting ride was ahead of us, as the wind was blowing over 25 mph and gusting more from the northeast. Fortunately, traffic was light as we were continually buffeted over the line. We climbed the very steep 122 foot bridge and then had to pedal hard to make progress down the other side. We seemed to find bridges in the morning, and bridges build character! For the first ten miles we headed north with good shoulders and then turned west from Alabama Port. The shoulders gave way to six-inch strips, which made it difficult to stay out of the driving lane as the panniers stuck out several more inches. Then the "sleeper lines" started. The shoulder area is milled or rolled to create rumble strips to alert a driver if he veers off the road. In Alabama, the entire shoulder is made into this; hence, you cannot ride on the shoulder. We were having a tough time with the heavy Saturday traffic. Combine that with very unfriendly drivers and we wanted out. We stopped for lunch in Bayou La Batre and then continued mile after uncomfortable mile. Soon, we were in Mississippi where these conditions continued. When we came to the town of Hurley, Mississippi at the junction of Hwy 613 and 614, we took a timeout to check our options. We had been on the road for over 7 1/2 hours and had only gone 50 miles because of the traffic and hills. The ACA map showed a possible campsite in another 20 miles, but I did not want to attempt another camp so soon. We studied our other map and GPS and decided that we would rather bike the Gulf Coast route and then head more northward. So we bailed from the ACA route and headed to Moss Point, Mississippi.

On the way, we had a strange encounter with a car. As the car passed us, the passenger stuck his arm out of the window and pointed across the street. We looked over, and there was a cemetery. Maybe he wanted to say we were going to die on this shoulderless road. This was very strange. We found an inexpensive motel next to a Domino's Pizza and a gas station. The pizza and beer made up for the exhausting and confusing day. The bonus was that I slept very well in the bed without the up and down pain. *I must be loosening up,* I thought. *It's either that or increased pain tolerance.*

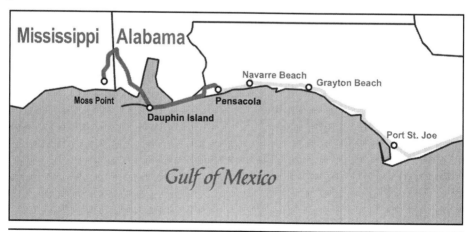

Day 12-Day 15: Pensacola, Florida to Moss Point, Mississippi

Chapter 7:
Coasting to and Through Louisiana

Day 16: A Nice Ride Through the
Mississippi Gulf Coast and into Louisiana
Sunday October 9, 2011; 88 miles –
Total so Far: 797 miles

We woke up, quickly packed, and had a nice, warm breakfast in the lobby. We sat with an older gentleman who had ridden cross country on a motorcycle with his new bride. He said they just gave up their motorcycle ten years ago due to an accident but really missed the freedom of the road that we were having. We could tell he wished he were in our shoes.

This turned out to be another morning for bridges. We traversed many double bridges to get to the coast. Several of them were very long, but the water scenery was nice. Most of the Gulf Coast ride was on very wide shoulders or on excellent beach walkways. We were very happy with the route we had chosen. Whenever possible, we stayed on the road and freely mixed with the traffic. It was Sunday and the last day of a coast-long car rally. But the drivers were very courteous and just out cruising. At the red lights, drivers would roll down their windows and talk to us. We were given many friendly honks (light taps) and thumbs up. The sun was out and we had a good tailwind, as we moved briskly along on this fun day. Some parts were sandy and made me nervous. I believed that if I fell again the trip would end.

We stopped at a sports bar for a sandwich and beer, and then we continued on until two guys stopped us and wanted to talk about our ride. One of the guys was planning a long trip and asked lots of bike questions. I gave them my contact card with websites and we rode on. About an hour later, we were on the beachside bike path when we came upon one of the guys again. He said he had to return and tell us he had just gone to my journal and that he was also born in Oxnard, was also 58 years old, and his name was Mike! So we compared notes about growing up in Oxnard, California. What a small world! He added comments to my Crazy Guy journal frequently through the finish of our trip. We did not have a map of Mississippi, so were just following the GPS. Mike told us that at our rate we should make Slidell, Louisiana on that day and gave us great directions. We stopped at the state line for pictures and entered Louisiana — our fourth state!

We had been on US 90 most of the day, but since that continues to New Orleans, where we did not want to go, especially on bicycles, we turned south onto US 190. Once we entered Louisiana, we passed many beautiful bayous. We stopped at several of them for pictures. We finally made it to the town of Slidell and had some backtracking to do parallel to the interstate until we found a decent motel and did our thing. Laundry was strung everywhere, as we had not done it the night before. The local food mart was our stop for dinner, beer, and the very important map of Louisiana. It's good to have a map, as we never know from one day to the next where we will be the next night. That was adventure to us. This conservative space shuttle engineer was completely out of his element and loving it!

Riding into Biloxi, Mississippi

A sandy bike path along the Gulf Coast

Day 17: A Rail-Trail Bike Path and then Back onto Hwy 190
Monday October 10, 2011; 60 miles –
Total so Far: 857 miles

I was up early to find a laundry, as our clothes were still damp. I found one about 1 1/2 miles away and put the clothes in the dryer. Jocelyn could use the extra rest, I figured. Breakfast consisted of yogurt and fresh fruit from Racetrac. The motel manager gave us directions to the local AAA office, so we stopped there and gathered maps for the remainder of our trip. As we were riding out of town on 190 without a shoulder, a driver caught up with us and said she wanted to talk. We pulled over and she pointed out the Tammany Trace Rail-Trail that runs parallel to 190. She said she wanted to do her good deed for the day, and she certainly did as this bike path ran for almost 30 miles. We enjoyed the leisurely ride with a small headwind. I was going too slowly for Jocelyn, and she told me so. My knee was hurting, but I think I was just being lazy. I picked up the pace and we rode through several small towns.

Lunchtime put us in Abita Springs, where we scored an excellent plate lunch of pulled pork, green beans, and carrots at a small local general store. We both commented that we were glad we didn't live here because of the food — we would eat too much! This was a typical Louisiana lunch box. We ate in a nearby park and then laid out on the lawn for a nap. At the end of the trail was the town of Covington, which was an extremely biker-unfriendly place, and it didn't help that it was rush hour and the schools had just let out. Once again there were no shoulders, and the sidewalks were broken up. In fact, we stopped at several places to ask directions and got several different answers. We decided to turn around but couldn't even cross the street until a lady just stopped the traffic with her car and allowed us to cross. She followed us and gave us the right directions to Hammond. The road signs, maps, and our GPS had totally confused us, but with her help we continued on the right course.

There were many times on our trip, in fact too many, where the GPS sent us on these out of the way roads to find our destination. There is a GPS selection of how you want to be directed; for example, it can give you the fastest route or the shortest route, but still at times it doesn't make sense. On this day, to get to our chosen motel, we were taken through neighborhoods where we weaved in and out instead of the more direct route around neighborhoods. We finally made it to a Best Western and settled into a nice room. Since there was a laundry room on the premises, we took advantage of that. Right next door was an excellent Mexican Restaurant that would be our first of many.

A Louisiana bayou

Day 18: Across the Great Mississippi River
Tuesday October 11, 2011; 75 miles –
Total so far: 932 miles

We had another confusing morning getting out of town because the GPS had put us so far off the main road. Sometimes I felt like the GPS owned us. We were not going to let that happen again. Once again we went through morning rush-hour traffic on our way out of Hammond. We continued west on Hwy 190. I was almost hit by a school bus while crossing a short shoulderless bridge. Jocelyn was ahead of me and over the bridge when the bus came up. The bus did not slow down or move over, even though the oncoming lane was clear. I really don't think the driver saw me. As I watched in my rear view mirror, I thought, *This is it — I'm gone.* So I looked straight ahead, closed my eyes, and waited for the impact — which did not occur. I felt like the rush lifted the bike up.

Other than that, it was a good morning. We stopped for lunch at Maria's Mexican Restaurant in Denham Springs, Louisiana. It was a good stop with good food, and we were the first customers of the day. We then powered our way through Baton Rouge, and I do mean 'powered', as in, "Let's get the heck out of here!" The traffic was bad and there was really nothing to look at as we cycled through the commercial district. The only good thing about this ride was the good shoulder. I couldn't imagine doing this otherwise.

In the Baton Rouge area there are only two ways to cross the Mississippi River: on the interstate I-10 or Hwy 190 which we were on. We had read that it is illegal to cross on I-10 (and we didn't want to be on I-10 anyway), so we continued on 190. We came up to the bridge but slowed down because there was no shoulder. Jocelyn had been riding back and yelled, "Just go!" I told her to take point. In situations like this I always told Jocelyn to go first, because if an errant driver drifted over, I would be the first hit and she would probably be okay. Hey, I figured that I've had a long and good life so far and that Jocelyn is just starting out. Along with that, I am larger and more visible than Jocelyn. Fortunately, traffic over the bridge was light. I gripped the handlebars and stared straight ahead. I did chance one glance to my left shoulder and saw downtown Baton Rouge and the I-10 Bridge. By the time we made it over, I exhaled a huge sigh of relief and was so elated to have crossed the mighty Mississippi! This was one of many great trip memories. There was a Circle K food mart on the right, so we stopped for a drink. I bought a 24 oz. tall boy beer, and the clerk put it in a paper bag. Once outside, I popped it open, gave Jocelyn the first drink, and then downed it. That was the first of my "stealth" beer drinking on the trip. I just had one, but it was so refreshing and it refreshed the ride.

We continued on 190 and rode by acres and acres of sugar cane fields. After several more miles the light was slowly disappearing, so I checked my GPS. There was a motel in Livonia, Louisiana about 15 miles ahead and nothing else, as towns were pretty sparse around here. As we entered Livonia close to dark, I could not spot a motel where the GPS put it. "Oh no," I told Jocelyn, "it must have closed." But we continued on, and there was the Oak Tree Inn. I became concerned because it was very small and the parking lot was full. I told Jocelyn, "We may be camping somewhere." There was one small room left that was fortunately on the bottom floor. The bikes barely fit. When we stepped back outside, I said, "This is perfect."

Jocelyn looked at me, puzzled, and I explained, "There is a gas station for beer and snacks, a restaurant, and a motel all in the same location." There was also a laundry on the premises. After I loaded the washing machine, I went back to the room to update Crazy Guy. Jocelyn was outside talking on the phone, and when she came back in I asked her to put the wash in the dryer when it was done. When I was finished I went out to bring in the clothes, but they were totally wet. I checked the washer and it had not completed the cycle. Jocelyn had just taken them out totally soaked! This was a definite sign of being tired and overworked. *We need a day off,* I thought. After a lot more time, the laundry was complete and we had dinner at Penny's Diner next door for another excellent meal.

During the meal, we noticed several people from the motel coming in and out and then leaving in vans. Come to find out, most of the rooms were taken by railroad workers who had been living here for a few months. Day shift had just ended and the night shift was taking off. In small towns we found a lot of places like this. Workers lived in the small, local motels because there were no other places available. We went back to the room and retired late. As there was only one small bed, I slept on a comfortable lounge chair.

Day 19: Some Hard West Miles with Strong Headwinds and Climbing
Wednesday, October 12, 2011; 82 miles – Total so Far: 1014 miles

The day started with a good breakfast at the diner, compliments of the motel. We traveled over the several-mile-long Morganza Spillway. None of the many bridges we crossed had shoulders, but the drivers were very accommodating. All of them, including lots of truckers, just moved over without honking. It was over one of the larger bridges that we saw our second touring biker of the trip. He was fully loaded and headed east. We would have loved to stop and talk with him, but there was no way to cross. So we just waved. The headwinds increased and we could feel ourselves climbing. After a few hours, we entered a small town that had a rest stop. This rest stop consisted of a porta potty, two picnic tables, and lots of big, shady trees. There was a small river next door, so while I investigated that, Jocelyn took a nap on one of the tables. We were both pretty beat and tired of the long days, and of course the headwinds didn't help matters. We still hadn't seen another motel or campsite since last night. I hesitated to try "stealth" camping because of Jocelyn. I don't know who we might encounter if we did. If I were alone I wouldn't hesitate at all.

After lunch in Eunice, Louisiana, we thought about spending the night there but it just seemed too early and we figured we could get many more miles in before dark. The next town of Kinder was 28 miles away, and we decided to go for it. At our riding speed, 28 miles was a little over two hours. About halfway there, the wind really picked up and we could see thunderstorms in the distance. I was really struggling. I'm sure Jocelyn was too, but she didn't show it. Jocelyn is like that and only really complains when she is hungry, as she needs her three square meals at the right time. I learned that really quickly! I can go on and on with little food, but she can't. Fortunately, all the rain and thunderstorms were parallel to us and heading east. We were only sprinkled on, but nonetheless we pushed our speed.

We stopped and took pictures of the town's welcoming sign: 'Welcome to Kinder: Crossroads to Everywhere'. It was after 6:00 P.M. and getting dark. We quickly picked out a motel not too far from the road and then stopped at a nearby grocery store and picked out fruit, juices, cereal, and beer. After that, we did the laundry and tried to figure out what restaurant to eat at. The selection was Mexican or Cajun. I knew we were both tired when we got into an argument, as Jocelyn wanted Mexican — again — while I wanted to try the Cajun. At this point I said, "Mexican it is." It was good. Back at the room, I did the everyday "duty" of Crazy Guy updating. I say "duty" because sometimes it was the last thing I wanted to do, as it felt like a real job sometimes. There were days when I just wanted to crawl into bed at the end of the day's ride and not get up until the next day. This was one of them. After the updates, I passed out.

Jocelyn: We have made it to Kinder, Louisiana. With 17 days down, we have gone a total of 1,014 miles! Minus the fact that we're both exhausted, we are looking forward to a day of rest! This happens to fall after my birthday on the 17th. What a great present, Dad! Thank you all for your support. I am grateful for all of the interest in what I am doing and amazed at the inspiration this is bringing with every peddle push, every mile, and every struggle.

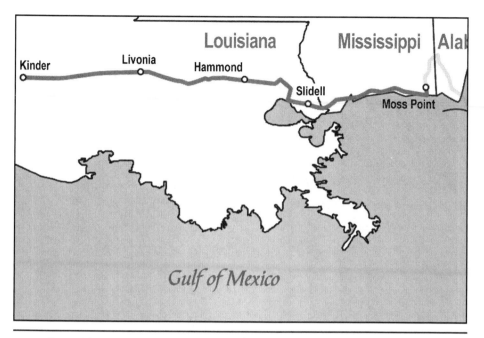

Day 16-Day 19: Moss Point, Mississippi to Kinder, Louisiana

Chapter 8:
Texas Climbing Maneuvers

Day 20: A Beautiful Ride Through the Hilly Forests of West Louisiana and Into Texas
Thursday October 13, 2011; 76 miles –
Total so Far: 1090 miles

We started the day with a fruit-filled breakfast and oatmeal thanks to the nearby grocery store. I had also bought my favorite drink, carrot juice. I had been putting off some needed bike repair and decided to get that done, so we got a late start at 9:30 A.M. Sometimes we needed those long mornings, even though it was not rest, as it kept us off the saddle a little longer. We both need a break but decided to wait until we were in a nicer area, as we didn't want to hang out where we were. We rejoined 190 West and had a nice ride through pine tree forests and fields of wildflowers. It was really beautiful and we stopped several times to take pictures. Eventually, Jocelyn was tired of stopping and said, "Dad, don't you have enough flower pictures?"

I replied, "No, it is all so beautiful."

We paralleled a railroad and watched two trains pass by. The hills were challenging but fun. What I didn't expect was all the derailleur problems on The Beast. The chain dropped several times and the shifting gave an awful noise. At the top of one hill I had a very difficult time setting the chain. Jocelyn kept asking if we need to return to Kinder and find a bike shop. This was the first time we both had our doubts about The Beast, and we weren't even halfway there yet. I finally got it working again, and we continued on to DeQuincy, Louisiana for lunch. We eventually left 190 and switched to LA 12 for our ride into Texas.

The entire part of the trip after the Mississippi River had been excellent shoulders and respectful drivers over dozens of bridges. We entered Texas and passed the welcoming sign of the State of Texas built out of concrete. Jocelyn climbed the sign and posed for several pictures, as were very happy to be here. Jocelyn was acting like she owned the state! Most bicyclists take about three weeks to cross Texas, so I told her, "Let's see how you feel three weeks from now!" We looked all around for a campground but did not find any. We wanted to head north and rejoin the ACA route, but that was about 25 miles north into a stiff headwind. Neither of us had the energy for that. According to the GPS, the city of Orange, Texas, along with several motels, was 10 miles south. It was out of the way, but with the wind it was a quick ride. We quickly found a motel complete with laundry. On one side was a quick mart for beer, and on the other was a Mexican restaurant. This was our favorite setup. After 76 miles, the tacos and ice-cold Dos Equis Amber beers were great. Jocelyn kept sneaking my beer, so I ordered a few extra. Tomorrow we would go northwest and rejoin the ACA trail, but for right now it was time for a long siesta.

Jocelyn: After leaving Sunny Florida seven days ago, we have crossed three states, traveled over a hundred bridges, picked up our average miles, have seen too many dogs chase us, and had one rather unkind passenger lift his hand over the top of the truck and clearly point to a cemetery across the road. We've been through towns with nothing but a bar, a few bad spots where one man yelled out to us, "I hate White people," and also experienced a lot of friendly and kind faces along the way. Of course they usually said we were crazy for doing such a thing. So now we have done it, made it to Texas, and we're pumped for this leg of the trip! We are expecting to be in Texas for maybe two weeks, and we're prepared to see what we will face in this Lone Star State!

The Texas state line

Day 21: Back on the ACA Map and an Oasis Appears Friday October 14, 2011; 50 miles – Total so Far: 1,140 miles

We were up early and walked to the main road for a quick breakfast, then to an ATM for cash. Since we'd had to backtrack, we got on the bikes and pushed on. We had to weave around construction near I-10 but eventually found ourselves heading north on Hwy 62 which would lead us to the ACA route. We stopped for a snack of sweet rolls and chocolate milk at a market in the middle of nowhere, and Jocelyn found a new friend, a very cute beagle puppy. They played for a bit while I studied the map and GPS. When it was time to go, the puppy wanted to follow us, so we asked a customer to hold him while we rode off as we didn't want him to run into the street.

We continued to climb north and ate lunch in Silsbee, Texas. At around 3:00 P.M., we were passing through the town of Kountze when we spotted a very nice-looking motel. We were both very tired and suffering from saddle sores. I looked at Jocelyn and she gave me the 'Let's stop' look. I didn't need any more convincing, so we pulled in and registered for one of the two remaining rooms. We were told that the "city people" came here to the country for the weekend. This Motel 8 had very large suites, and for the price of $55 it was a real deal! The bikes were lost in the large room. Across the street was a food mart, so we loaded up with dinner food and beer as there were no restaurants nearby and we were done riding for the day. I did the laundry and Jocelyn hung out by the pool and napped while I worked on The Beast some more. We were done with everything by 6:00 P.M. Now what? It didn't take long to settle down with some chips and beer while watching TV. I was soon bored by the TV and got out the ACA map and the Texas map. The ACA route took us north more through the countryside with lots of camping available. It was also very hilly and winding. With The Beast acting up, we decided to head southwest and leave the hill country. We hadn't seen a bike shop since Pensacola, and at this point The Beast needed some professional help.

Day 22: Off the ACA Route Again and a Westerly Ride Through Ranchlands Saturday October 15, 2011; 83 miles – Total so Far: 1,223 miles

Once again we decided to go off the ACA map and go out on our own. After a nice motel breakfast, we tried to get an early start but several of the guests stopped us for questions as we walked the bikes out through the lobby. They all seemed to have a biker in their family and wanted pictures with us. We happily obliged and then headed out of Kountze to Hwy 770 which led to Hwy 105. This route parallels the ACA route but about 20 miles south. We had nothing but good roads and shoulders as we passed many ranches. We were also chased by about 30 dogs! The last one almost got Jocelyn. She was unclipped and ready to kick when I rang my bell and once again the dog came right at me. I squeezed my water bottle at him and that startled him just enough for us to get away. We would remember that for next time. Some of the dogs seem trained enough to stop the chase when their property ended, and most did not cross from the other side, but there are exceptions to every rule. We did carry pepper spray for dogs and humans. Before we left, many people asked us what we were carrying, as in guns. They were always surprised when I said, "Nothing."

We passed three dead deer on the shoulder. I was tempted to stop and take a few pictures, but it was too gruesome. We had heard that hunting season started in a few weeks and a good season was expected because of the drought. We had noticed timed deer feeders for sale at many stores along the road. They are set up on hunting properties and set to attract deer so that when the season starts there are deer hanging out for the hunter. This seemed a little strange to us non-hunters.

We had a good but late lunch in Cleveland (Texas, not Ohio!) after a morning 50 mile run. Our choice today was The Plantation Mexican Americana Buffet. The parking lot was packed so we figured it must be a good local place. It was an incredible Mexican and Texas barbeque, all you can eat lunch buffet for only $8. There wasn't any beer, so I settled for my first soda of the trip and that was included too. This is an excellent stop for bikers, as we could really pig out and eat all we wanted, because the calories are quickly burned. One of Jocelyn's friends texted her, "Are you still in Texas?" Jocelyn texted back, "We are having lunch in Cleveland." At this her friend replied, "What-what!" Jocelyn got her on that one. We were so fueled that we put another 30 miles on the odometer.

We figured this must be hay country since we saw many rolled up hay bales on trucks. This was something you don't see at the beach in Cape Canaveral! We were so interested in the hay that we stopped and took many pictures of hay and trucks. Jocelyn wanted them. And yet she had made comments when I took all those wildflower pictures a few days before. We also saw upcoming billboards such as Cut and Shoot Hardware. *Must be a joke,* I thought. But sure enough, we came up to the Cut and Shoot Volunteer Fire Department and the Cut and Shoot Post Office. This was the strangest town name we saw the entire trip. I know there must be a story there somewhere. It sounds like the name of a horror movie.

We entered the city of Conroe, Texas where a weekend festival resulted in very heavy traffic. The first two motels were booked. After going out of our way south a few miles, we found a room. Once again there was road construction around the nearby interstate, so the riding was challenging with heavy traffic. Sometimes at the end of the day it was so frustrating to get where we wanted to stay, and this day was no exception. It was then another mile on the bikes back through heavy traffic to find something to eat. We were once again exhausted.

Day 23: "Where in the Heck Are We?" or "Where Did All These Hills Come From?" Sunday October 16, 2011; 79 miles – Total so Far: 1,302 miles

We woke up thinking about how Jocelyn would be celebrating her 21st birthday tomorrow! We had wanted to celebrate in Austin, Texas, but that was too distant at this point, especially since we were headed into

"Texas Hill Country". We left at 8:00 A.M. and stopped at Home Depot for a few supplies on our way out of town, and once again we were on Hwy 105. We rode up and down large hills, and five hours later we had only managed 40 miles. The Beast and I were having a really tough time, and I was having breathing problems. My broken rib was talking to me, and I heard it loud and clear. We needed a day off the bikes. We stopped in Navasota, Texas for lunch and talked with a local trucker who just smiled when I talked about all the hills.

"The hills are just starting," he laughed.

"Great!" I added.

"Remember, Dad," Jocelyn reminded me, "that you said hills build character."

I replied, "Yes, and so does resting."

The trucker said that a mere 25 miles from here was Brenham, Texas where there were nice motels. So Brenham it was. After a good barbeque lunch, we were on our way.

We continued on Hwy 105 through the hills and heat. None of our preparation in Florida could have prepared us for this. We exhausted another five hours on the bikes. Our average speed was less than 10 mph as we rode over increasingly larger hills. The elevation of the steep hills was 250-350 feet with the largest at almost 400 feet. It was really hard riding, and I was now worried about what the future held for The Beast and me. Jocelyn just pedaled along smoothly while I clanged away, wincing at each shift. My left side throbbed. We hadn't come to any mountains yet, and "West Texas Canyon Country" would soon appear. We stopped at a quick mart for a beer and powered through to Brenham. Once there, we were again totally confused between the motel road signs and the GPS. Unfortunately, we followed the GPS and got lost on the other side of town. The traffic was so heavy that it took us several minutes just to cross the road and return to town. We just could not figure out where the motels were. Jocelyn suggested heading south on the freeway and that we should run into something soon. We had yet to ride on a freeway, but there is a first time for everything and we were desperate. We rode onto the Hwy 290 on-ramp and joined the crowd of cars and trucks. A few miles later, we left the 290 off-ramp to find several nice motels. The hill work continued just to get up to the Hampton Inn. As I checked in at this very nice motel, I thought, *Break time!*

"Two nights please," I said to the clerk. We had spent 10 1/2 hours on the saddle for a mere 79 miles. We were totally exhausted. Once we cleaned up, we walked to the local Applebee's for a late dinner. It was good and we slept well.

Quote of the day from Jocelyn: "I'm using my gears now, Dad!"

Monday October 17, 2011; Jocelyn's 21st Birthday! Happy Birthday, Princess!

I kind of thought we would be in Texas for this momentous occasion. It would be a different birthday for Jocelyn because I was the only one here to help her celebrate. We slept in this huge, beautiful studio. At 8:30 we went to the lounge for a delicious breakfast and planned the day. Jocelyn wanted to hang out at the pool, as in "really rest", and I wanted to strip the bikes clean of all grease and crud on the gears and chains. We wheeled the bikes out back, and I went to work with the degreaser I had bought from Home Depot in Conroe. My bike was filthy, but Jocelyn's was still pretty clean. Before we left home, I had cleaned both bikes' chains and gears, so I don't know why mine was so dirty. Perhaps it was all the shifting.

Both bikes cleaned up well, and I lubed them with a small amount of oil on the chains. Jocelyn had a small leak on her front tire, so I patched the tube. I put everything back together, cleaned up, and gave them a test ride. It was so much fun riding around the hilly motel property without panniers. I kept riding around and around while shifting through all the gears. The Beast was working better. I then jumped on Jocelyn's Surly and rode it around. What a nice bike! Jocelyn had been at the pool watching me as I made the circuit. She finally got up and said, "Dad, what are you doing? This is a break day."

"Just having fun, Jocelyn," I replied, and I certainly was. It's funny that this was a break day and I was already thinking about tomorrow.

We cleaned up and went to Applebee's again for lunch, except this time we sat at the bar and both of us ordered a draft beer. I was so glad, and Jocelyn was very happy when she was carded. I even took a picture! After all, it was her first legal drink. We had an excellent lunch and talked with the bartenders and wait staff about our trip. They were all very interested and amazed. One of the bartenders made Jocelyn a few special drinks on the house. I stuck with the beer. After lunch I retired to the room for a nap, while Jocelyn went back to the pool. It was a nice warm and sunny day. We then went to Chili's for dinner where Jocelyn was carded again. She was happy. We walked through Walmart on the way back to the Hampton Inn for some birthday ice cream. We retired early, dreaming of keeping the wheels going "round and round".

Jocelyn: We are in Brenham, Texas! Such a nice size town at the nicest hotel yet and a great present from my dad — a rest day on my birthday! Today is my 21st birthday. Of course birthdays are just tallies, because I am always changing and growing by the day, not by the year. The hills are here as an early present too. I am riding strong, but my dad is really showing some struggling with them. We just can't wait to hit the mountains! Really loving Texas though; the country is amazing; the sun is hot; the wind is blowing, and now the beer is flowing!

Day 24: Our Worst Day of Wind Yet
Tuesday October 18, 2011; 42 miles –
Total so Far: 1,344

I was up early and looked outside. I couldn't see more than a few feet beyond the window. I walked outside to find that we were completely fogged in with the first fog of our trip. When I returned to the room, I told Jocelyn, "Go back to sleep. It is too foggy to ride." She seemed happy about that. I sat around for an hour or so and then went outside again. The fog was lifting, but it was extremely windy and coming from the direction we needed to go. *This is going to be a long day,* I thought.

We then went to breakfast and started riding. We had to backtrack a few miles on the freeway with the wind at 20-30 mph with 40 mph gusts! I had bought a wind gauge for the trip, but every time I used it, all it had was bad news for us. Anybody could tell that it was windy. I really didn't need to know the speed! We finally made it back to the Hwy 290 West intersection. As we turned west, I thought that we might have some tailwind, but we were still being headed. After 20 miles, we took Hwy 237 southwest which gave us some extreme crosswinds on this two-lane road. It was a real struggle to stay on the shoulder or even in the entire lane for that matter. Both of us were struggling and not talking. Jocelyn pulled over a few times and just stood there. I did the same.

We had chosen this route, as we decided to not visit Austin but instead to go to San Antonio. The countryside was really beautiful. The hill work was okay, but there is absolutely nothing you can do about the wind. At least you can attack and work a hill, but the wind is nothing but a brute force to be reckoned with. I told Jocelyn, "Wind builds character." From the look on her face, she told me what I could do with the wind! Just when all seemed to come to a grinding halt, we rode into the tiny town of Warrenton and stopped at an old store, Warrenton Grocery, hoping to find a sandwich.

This stop ended up being another oasis for us. When we walked in, I asked the lady behind the counter if there were any sandwiches available. She said, "We only sell freshly made sandwiches; what kind can I make for you?" We placed an order with her and walked around and gathered a few Lone Star beers and chips and sat down at a table. We popped open the beers and felt so relieved from leaving the wind. Soon, Doris brought over our ham sandwiches and gave us the history of the town. Her grocery store was built in 1854, and she and her husband were only the third owners! So we talked about that and our trip. Whenever we wanted something, we just walked around and brought it back to the table to eat. She reminded me a lot of my mom. She was very interested in our trip and was asking many detailed questions. Doris made us feel at home and brought Jocelyn and me back on speaking terms. Doris could not believe that we were riding bicycles in, "this awful wind." She said to us, "There is a motel in La Grange, about 10 miles down the road. You need to get out of this wind." That sounded great to us, so we followed her advice and found the Best Western in La Grange, Texas. There were no restaurants nearby, but we called a local food mart that delivered to us a delicious Texas barbeque dinner. It had only been a 42-mile day, but it was still progress. That night when we went to bed, the wind continued to howl, and it never did calm down.

Day 25: Some More of the Old H & H (Hills and Headwinds)
Wednesday October 19, 2011; 72 miles – Total so Far: 1,416 miles

After another good motel breakfast, we got an early start and were immediately challenged by the headwind. The crosswinds that we had encountered toward the end of yesterday's ride had shifted on us. We rode through downtown La Grange and were greeted by the 550 foot Monument Hill as we left town. Jocelyn flew by me as I struggled with The Beast. I had to walk part of the climb. It was not all The Beast, as I just wasn't in large hill-climbing shape yet. That would come soon though.

We continued through the beautiful countryside scattered with many ranches. The cattle were plentiful, and we lost count of all the different kinds of cows and steers. I was into the habit of ringing my bike bell whenever we rode by animals, and the cows always seemed to look up. I wondered what they were thinking. I remembered the old "Far Side" cartoon that shows cows standing on their hind legs and chatting. When a car approaches, one cow yells, "Car," and they all get down on four legs and stare. Most horses get scared and run away. We also enjoyed stopping and taking pictures of all the ornamental ranch gates with some very elaborate artwork.

We stopped for lunch at Brenda's Place in Flatonia, Texas. This bar and grill serves an excellent grilled cheese sandwich and, of course, ice cold Lone Star. We met "Mr. Brenda" who told us the history of Flatonia and gave us some good information about riding through West Texas. In his younger days, he had traveled by motorcycle so he knew the road well. It was 40 miles more to Luling, Texas and the next accommodations. Mr. Brenda said, "You are now entering East Texas Hill Country, so good luck."

I cringed at that.

The large hills seemed endless with one after another. Along with that, the wind just beat us down. For a while I had second thoughts about this trip. Cary had added some of what he calls "Glorious Music" to my iPod. It is orchestral music from big movie themes. So I cranked up the music on this lonely road. It was a fight for every one of those 40 miles. But we did make it and were much stronger for it. When we rolled into Luling after 6:00 P.M., I was thinking, *Bring it on. I am ready for more!* I had really pushed myself. My throbbing legs felt great.

We immediately found a nice motel. I asked the manager for directions to the nearest restaurant, and he said, "Two miles away. I can take you." Wow, what service! He drove us to his favorite restaurant and gave us his phone number. "Just call when you are done," he said. After another excellent barbeque dinner, we were soon back in our room. As I have said several times, this trip is all about the people you meet and how some really go out of their way to help. As I went to sleep, I thought about San Antonio — tomorrow!

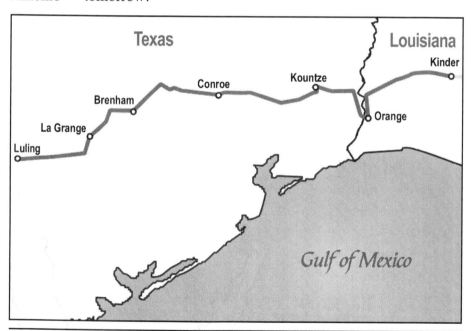

Day 20-Day 25: Kinder, Louisiana to Luling, Texas

Chapter 9:
San Antonio Repair Procedures

Day 26: We Cross Texas One Taco at a Time and Arrive in San Antonio
Thursday October 20, 2011; 40 miles – Total so Far: 1,456 miles

---

We had noticed that many Mexican restaurants in Texas are open for breakfast, so when we rode into downtown Luling we stopped at Mr. Taco. We each had the excellent *huevos rancheros*. We couldn't finish it all but were totally fueled for the day's ride. As we rode out of town, we noticed that Jocelyn had another front flat. We turned around to a gas station with an air hose and replaced the tube. Once again there was a small, thin wire from someone's shredded steel-belted tire in her tube. These shredded tires are scattered on the roadside shoulders. Neither of us were happy about the flat, but what can you do? All that it takes is one small piece to pierce the tire and tube. It is easy to avoid the shredded tire chunks, but what lurks on the shoulder are tiny broken-off pieces that really can't be seen. The one thing about the Surly that I didn't like was the tires. They are not as thick and sturdy as my Schwalbe Marathon Plus touring tires. This was Jocelyn's second flat.

When we had returned to our bikes in Port St. Joe, Florida after our trip to California, her back tire was flat, but we later found out from a bike shop that it wasn't a real flat as we had used a CO2 cartridge to inflate it while in Perry, Florida. According to this Panama City Beach bike shop owner, CO2 will permeate through a tube and it will be flat a few weeks later. We didn't know that, so we rethought our inflation practice.

The winds clocked around from the south, which gave us headwinds again though not as strong as the previous two days. This led to the old H&H. We passed through many old towns and railroad construction areas with an assortment of strange-looking machinery that is used to build and repair railroads. I have always enjoyed train stuff, so seeing this equipment was a photo op. We also passed a concrete drain factory that had several acres of drains stacked high and long. Once again I stopped for a few pictures. I think Jocelyn was getting tired of me stopping for all these pictures. "There's Dad again, lollygagging around!" she would say.

After a few steep hill climbs, we arrived in Sequin, Texas at lunchtime. We passed several nice-looking Mexican restaurants but weren't interested until we came upon Taqueria All Meat Tacos in an old converted gas station. Taqueria is an authentic Mexican roadside stand full of real Mexican food! We stuffed ourselves with an assortment of tacos and sauces along with homemade lemonade. The outside table was warm and sunny and found us talking with the owner and the workers about our trip. They were all very interested, so I gave one my card. Only one person there seemed to know anything about computers, and I wonder if he ever looked at our journal. It was still another 30 miles to San Antonio. We said goodbye.

West of Sequin, Hwy 90 is incorporated onto I-10, so we followed the GPS and wound up on an I-10 on-ramp. We didn't like this at all, so I climbed up the hillside and asked directions from a local business. The old Hwy 90 runs parallel right next to I-10 all the way to the city. That was good news, as we pretty much had the road to ourselves. It was exciting riding west, seeing the city of San Antonio rise from the land. This would be our first major city.

Once near the city, however, we did have to get on I-10 for the last two miles. It was a bit scary, but we rode right into downtown and found a very nice room in a Holiday Inn Express. I wanted a bike shop to look at The Beast, and I have always wanted to see the Alamo and the River Walk area of downtown. Many years ago, my parents had a wonderful time staying there and always encouraged us to visit. "Perfect time!" I said, and Jocelyn agreed. "It's another day off!" we declared. It was late again, so we cleaned up and walked a few blocks to — what else — but another Mexican restaurant. Another great meal was enjoyed along with several fine Texas brews. We wandered back to the hotel thinking of a nice, long sleep, and we certainly enjoyed that too!

San Antonio: Friday October 21, 2011: Break Day

I was up early checking the Internet for local bike shops. There were many here, so I started making phone calls. I explained my situation and finally got in contact with one that was relatively close: The Blue Star Bicycling Company. They seemed very accommodating and said to bring in my bike. While stripping it down, I decided to also take the Surly in and see if they had any better tires for it. We walked the bikes down to the parking lot. The taxi van I had called had arrived. It seemed like we were only about six miles from the shop, but I am glad we took the van just to save time. Once at the shop, I talked with the mechanic and he told me he would have it ready late the next morning. He also found two better tires for the Surly and would mount those for us along with cleaning and lubing both bikes. I was hoping that the mechanic would find something wrong with The Beast. Jocelyn and several others who were reading my journal on Crazy Guy had suggested that I get a new bike and ditch The Beast. The mechanic, however, suggested I stick with my ride even though he would love to sell me a new bike.

We left the bike shop and enjoyed a leisurely walk back to the downtown area by way of the River Walk. The San Antonio River twists and turns its way through downtown. Overlooking the river are many hotels, condos, and restaurants. Along with that, the river is navigated by open tourist boats. It really is beautiful and so different than anything I have ever seen. We had a nice riverside lunch that included talking to the waiter and chef. They are both bikers so we swapped some cool stories, and then I gave them my card. We had an important chore to do back at the hotel: get rid of more stuff. This time we mailed off eleven more pounds of stuff we hadn't yet used. My neighbor, Chris, had joked with me that the shoes I "just had" to bring would not get used. He was right; I hadn't even thought of them. Chris had looked at all the stuff that we were packing and laughed. "You'll be sending that home too," he laughed. By the time we reached San Diego, Jocelyn and I would be experts in packing.

After our trip to the post office, the first post office I have ever been to where we had to empty our pockets and go through a metal detector, we left in search for the Alamo. Our self-tour of the Alamo was a very moving experience. We were in awe of what those men went through to defend the fort. The large sculptured monument in front has all their names carved along with several of the leaders' figures. When we left the Alamo, we went to a local mall to chill at a movie. Then, it was another riverside Mexican dinner and the walk back to the hotel. The city was just coming alive, but we were ready for a rest. It had been a long but satisfying day.

Jocelyn: We have been hanging out in San Antonio, Texas for a day of rest, and my dad needed a tune-up on his bike. It's currently at Blue Star Bicycling Company, and we have been walking along the River Walk. Such a neat scenic adventure with many sights of people, restaurants, ducks, and — The Alamo! Hopefully, we will be on our way to the border tomorrow. We're projecting that it will take two days to get to Del Rio, Texas. I am ready to charge into the desert ahead!

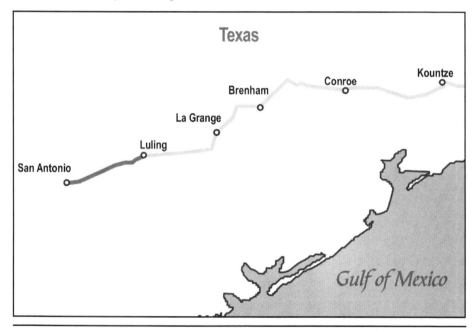

Day 26: Luling, Texas to San Antonio, Texas

Bike repair in San Antonio

Chapter 10:
Continued Climbing Maneuvers
to El Paso

Day 27: An Afternoon Ride Out of San Antonio with a Sunset Arrival in Hondo, Texas
Saturday October 22, 2011; 43 miles –
Total so Far: 1,499 miles

We spent the morning lounging around the hotel and napping while waiting for our bikes. I crossed the street for a haircut. We then piled all our panniers and gear onto the hotel's valet cart and waited for another taxi ride. As we waited, I played with the valet cart like it was a skateboard full of gear and scooted my way around the parking lot. I cried out, "I don't need no stinking bike! I'll ride this cart to California!" We had a good laugh over that. The taxi arrived and we were soon at the shop. The mechanic had not found any major problem with The Beast but cleaned it up and adjusted the derailleurs. I had not known about any adjustments, so it was good information for me. He had also cleaned it way better than I had back in Brenham. The Surly was sporting thicker and heavier tires. The original tires that he removed were already falling apart with many cuts and cracks. We were shocked since these tires only had 1,500 miles on them. In comparison, my Schwalbes had almost 4,000 miles and were still looking good! The new tires weren't as good as the Schwalbes, but they would have to do.

The Surly's chain and gears were also cleaned. There was a festival at a nearby park with lots of people wandering around the many shops. Once again we were besieged with questions and pictures. Since it was after lunch, we stepped next door to the Blue Star Brewing Company and sampled some fine home brew and excellent sandwiches. After that, we didn't want to leave and maybe we shouldn't have.

We finally left San Antonio at 3:30 and soon found ourselves on I-10. We had talked with the shop owner and were told that I-10 was the only way out unless you backtracked through downtown and went around the other side of the city. At this point we wanted out, so we went with I-10. Hwy 90 and I-10 are together here, so we worked our way through many on and off-ramps to keep going. Sometimes we actually ran our bikes across lanes after stopping for traffic. It was really bad. Fortunately, The Beast was shifting smoothly up and down the numerous ramps and overpasses and we were very focused and stressed out at this point. Finally, after six miles of this mess, I-10 split off to the west while we continued south on the lesser traffic of Hwy 90. It was peace at last. The shoulders were clean and the hills enjoyable. We soon found ourselves in a race against the sunset and continued to push ourselves, as we didn't want to be caught at night in the middle of nowhere. We finally pulled into a motel in Hondo, Texas right at sunset. That was too close but nonetheless a very satisfying 43 miles. We grabbed some food at a nearby food mart and talked about Del Rio to the south. It was only 100 miles and we decided to go for it the next day. But there were other plans in the works.

Day 28: Two New Tires and Two Flats, or Jocelyn Needs to Watch the Road Better Sunday October 23, 2011; 43 miles – Total so Far: 1,542 miles

We awoke to two flats on the Surly's two new tires! What a disappointment and surprise. After breakfast at the Regency Motel in Hondo, we removed the wheels and tires and found that a steel wire had penetrated each new tire through the sidewalls. My Schwalbes hadn't had a flat yet and we were riding the same shoulder. It must have been the tires, because you just can't see the tiny broken wires scattered along the shoulder. So far, Jocelyn had four flats all from wire pieces. Of these two, one was left in the tire/tube but the other could not be found, as often the wire will penetrate like a stingray barb and then spring out if it is connected to a larger piece. We changed out the tubes and then patched them. The gas station air next door wasn't working, so I pumped it up and spotted another gas station. This air station didn't work either. We have bicycle pumps that are advertised to pump high pressure, but we have yet to get a tire pumped above 60 pounds even though it is rated for twice that. I like keeping all the tires inflated to 70 psi to decrease rolling resistance with the heavy loads.

As we rode out of town, there was a Walmart auto center where I borrowed their air hose and topped off all the tires. I would also say that nine times out of ten the gas station/food mart air stations don't work. We had wasted a lot of coins in these machines because of their leaky nozzles, and this can be very frustrating when you need air. As a result of all this, we didn't get out of town until 11:30, which was way too late for a Del Rio, Texas run.

We continued our ride southwest on Hwy 90 and stopped for another excellent barbeque lunch at Grandpa Rudy's Pit Barbecue in Sabinal, Texas. Grandpa Rudy's is just a small single room metal shack but full of good food and great service. We were given way too much food but ate it anyway. Back on the road, there were many trains that passed us and as we gave the engineers the "blow your whistle" sign with our right arms, several complied. We were stoked. What a hoot! At 4:30 we rode into Uvalde, Texas and looked at our options. We had only gone 43 miles and the next accommodations were 40 more miles in Brackettville. Sunset was at 6:50, so that would give us 2 1/2 hours to go those 40 miles. It was doable because of the small hills and only a light headwind. But then I spotted a Holiday Inn Express and Applebee's. "I'm calling it a day, Jocelyn, unless you have any objections."

Jocelyn smiled and responded, "That makes two of us, Dad." We did a full load of laundry and then went across the street to Applebee's. It was football season, so we sat at the bar for dinner and chilled with some ice-cold drafts. I turned to Jocelyn and said, "This is living. We are very fortunate to be on this trip and enjoying ourselves with good food, beer, and nice accommodations." We were still carrying 25 pounds of camping gear, but at that moment, I didn't care.

Day 29: A Roller Coaster Ride into Del Rio
Monday October 24, 2011; 74 miles –
Total so Far: 1,616 miles

We left Uvalde early and pedaled into a nice Texas countryside. At first the road and shoulder were smooth, but it slowly turned rough and bumpy. Then the hills appeared and the ride became a continuous up and down with a vibration from the bumpy shoulder. The traffic was light, so we spent a lot of time left of the shoulder line. We found out later that many Texas roads are made from chip-seal which is a process of putting down a layer of tar and throwing rocks on top. These rocks stick to the tar, and that's the road. The problem is when larger than pebble-sized rocks are used. Over time, the tar shrinks away leaving a bumpy surface. Some of the shoulders are so bumpy that your teeth rattle! We were also told that the smaller the rock, the costlier the road. Hence, a poorer county will have a bumpier road. We did pass several work crews reworking the roads with regular asphalt. I would imagine that most of Hwy 90 from San Antonio to Del Rio is much smoother now.

This was another picture day for ornamental ranch gates. They were everywhere! People put a lot of pride into their ranches here. We also saw many sheep and goat farms and a few exotic animal farms with several species of antelope. There were also hunting ranches where hunters pay to hunt exotic animals. Since the ranch is fenced in, there is only so far that an animal can run from a hunter. It looks like a big business here. We did see several antelopes right inside the fence.

It was a scorching day, and we stopped several times for a rest. There was no water available since we left Uvalde, so when we rode into Brackettville we were almost empty. Jocelyn carries three 24 oz. bottles along with a 70 oz. waist pack, while I carry two 24 oz. bottles and a 100 oz. backpack. There were two restaurants in town, and we picked — you guessed it — the Mexican one! We each had a huge taco plate along with two ice-cold sodas. It was another oasis that we needed because we had another 30 miles into Del Rio.

On the way to the Best Western in downtown Del Rio, we came across Lakeside Sports Bike Shop. We went in and I immediately saw my Schwalbe Marathon-Plus Touring tires. I had been thinking about new ones, as the middle tread had been wearing away and we had another 500 miles or so of chip-seal to travel. I like these tires so much that I decided to replace Jocelyn's two day old tires with Schwalbes also. This shop is on the ACA route, and the owner said he sells a lot of them.

We found the Best Western down the street, checked in, stripped the bikes, and rode them back to Lakeside Sports to change out all four tires and tubes. We were told that they would be ready by 11:00 A.M. the next day. We walked back to the motel and went swimming in the pool even though the water was a bit cool. We enjoyed it immensely. After that, we found another good Mexican restaurant and then a long, restful sleep followed.

A hot ride into Del Rio, Texas

Day 30: A Tailwind Ride through Texas Canyon Country
Tuesday October 25, 2011; 33 miles – Total so Far: 1,649 miles

I was up early to find a laundry about a block away. The shop didn't open until 10:00 A.M., so we had a leisurely breakfast and caught up with our web site updates. At 11:00 A.M., we were at the shop admiring our new Schwalbes and trying to decide which of the older tires to keep as spares. We had been carrying an old one from home but decided to leave that at the shop and have two spares, one of my old Schwalbes and one of the new two-day-old Surly tires. I know that I over thought this, but that's the engineer in me. Back at the motel, we again had to reload everything on the bikes, which at this point was really getting old. On the way out of town, we stopped for lunch and then had another late start at 1:30. But the good news was that we had a very nice tailwind, our first in Texas!

We passed Amistad National Recreation Area which includes a huge lake with lots of boating. At first we thought it odd that the bike shop was named "Lakeside", but now we knew why. After the lake, we had a beautiful ride through cut rock canyons, cactus, and fields of purple flowers. We soon climbed to an easy 1,600 feet — we had our climbing legs at last! We were flying through Canyon Country enjoying 30 mph down the grades. That in itself is scary because of the fully-loaded panniers. One time we went through a pass and watched as a train passed by many miles away. I thought we were in the old west! The Beast was shifting okay but still making so much grinding noise that it started to bother me again, while the Surly was smoothly cruising along. At the top of one steep hill was the tiny town of Comstock, Texas. As per our routine, we stopped to see our options. There was a campground without facilities about 10 miles further west, a motel in Sanderson (another 82 miles), and a really cool-looking mom and pop motel to our left. This was another no-brainer, so we checked in to the Comstock Motel and immediately walked across the street for some beer and snack food. The manager said that they did get a lot of bicycle traffic because they are on the Adventure Cycling Association route. The small bar/cafe across the street didn't open until 6:00 P.M. so I did the laundry in the bucket and Jocelyn stretched out in the warm sun. We asked the waitress at J&J Holley's Place Cafe and Bar to bring us the best thing on the menu. Soon, we were each eating an excellent cheeseburger washed down with delicious Shiner Bock beer. After dinner, we hung out at the cool bar decorated with an old Western theme, including Indian statues and John Wayne pictures. Tomorrow we would have a real challenge. The next town was Sanderson with a climb to 3,000 feet. We retired early as we wanted to be on the road at sunrise.

Jocelyn: We have had quite a past few days full of chip seal shoulders (rocks spread over tar, not pushed down or flattened out), plenty of Mexican food (Yes, I think I really am done with all of this food on the trip. Man, it is too good and too much!), and interesting small towns. Oh, and also both my dad and I faced our first experience of "survival mode" with no water and plenty of sun. We were riding to Del Rio, Texas, and water was sparse. I had to limit myself to 3 sips of water for every 15 minutes. I found myself staring at the clock when I had five more minutes left till my next sip of water, and that five minutes seemed like an hour. But for now, I am focused on tomorrow and how tough it will be through desert conditions and the "tallest" bridge in Texas all the way to Sanderson, Texas along the border of Mexico. 88 miles total, wish us luck.

Day 31: A Climbing Day to Sanderson, and The Beast Breaks
Wednesday October 26, 2011; 90 miles – Total so Far: 1,739 miles

We were up early and ate the breakfast food we bought yesterday. At first light we were on the road out of Comstock. It was a beautiful morning with a bright sunrise, and we watched a train speed by in the distance. We stopped and took several pictures as we steadily climbed through many canyons and enjoyed magnificent vistas. As a bonus, there was no car or truck traffic for the first hour or so. What a nice biking route! I kept looking for a stagecoach or Indians on the horizon. If there is such a thing as total peace, we found it this morning when we crossed the Pecos River. We stopped and were in awe of this beautiful river that empties into the Rio Grande. The bridge used to be one of the tallest in the world at 321 feet above the river. We heard nothing except the wind and an occasional sheep bleating. To the south was Mexico. There were many border patrol trucks cruising the road. They were all very friendly and waved as we rode by.

We soon arrived at the small town of Langtry, Texas and stopped for lunch at the Langtry Depot. Inside, there were many signs that advertised their "Delicious Barbeque Sandwich". Since there was nothing else on the menu, we both had one — and it *was* delicious. The largest dog I have ever seen soon appeared and walked up to Jocelyn. We were seated at a table and Gus' head was higher than Jocelyn's. That was one big dog! Our goal of Sanderson was 60 miles ahead, so we didn't stay long.

Jocelyn was in her speed mood and would charge ahead and disappear. There were several "No Services" rest stops along this route. I would always catch up with her as she would lie on a picnic table and take a siesta while waiting for me. The Beast and I were just clanking along. At one point I saw her way ahead with three Billy goats in pursuit. There were two border patrolmen laughing on the side as I passed. The goats appeared scared when I caught up with them. They stopped and we continued, and then they ran after both of us. They soon tired and we were on our own again.

About 10 miles from the small town of Dryden, my chain once again dropped off the chainwheel and jammed in the gears. I wasn't prepared for this type of breakdown and thought, *Now what?* I was finally able to release it, but several inches of the chain was twisted. This was not good. I was still able to ride, although without shifting and very slowly. I figured from all the noise that the twisted chain was probably bending the gears. We crawled into Dryden, which had no services or accommodations. There were people headed to Sanderson, but their trucks were full of hay and alfalfa. There wasn't much traffic at all. We had 20 miles to go, and it was about an hour to sunset. Since the traffic was so light, I decided that we needed to get going. Jocelyn was not happy with that decision, but there was a motel in Sanderson and a bike shop in the town after that. So we both crawled along.

Climbing was tough without shifting, and I ended up walking some. At this point, I hadn't thought of manually moving the chain. It was canyon after canyon. In all my years of biking, this was probably the most challenging 20 miles. After dark, we slowly pedaled into the Budget Motel parking lot after a very stressful afternoon. The motel looked closed, but soon Danny, the manager, appeared in the parking lot and greeted us. He saw how stressed out we were and led us to his office and gave us a cold bottle of water. We told him our predicament with The Beast. According to the ACA map and Lakeside Sports Bike Shop, there was a bike shop in Alpine another 83 miles down the road. I asked him if he knew anyone with a truck that could take us there. Danny said he would call around and suggested a restaurant within walking distance. We checked in, parked our bikes, and walked to another Mexican restaurant. Again I thought to myself, *We truly are crossing Texas one taco at a time!*

On the way back, we picked up a six pack of beer and met Danny at the room. He found a friend to take us the next day as long as we paid the gas. Danny also kindly gave us the use of the motel laundry. We were soon asleep after finishing that. It had been a long 90 mile day of canyon riding with 30 miles of those with a twisted chain and no shifting. It looked like the next day we would miss out on 83 miles of riding. A purest would make that up, but I decided that we would hopefully continue from Alpine. It would all depend on whether The Beast could make it. I hoped the bike shop would be open the next day and that they would have a new chain and rear gear cluster.

Peace at the Pecos River

Day 32: We Hitched a Ride to Alpine, and Then it was a Short 31 Mile Ride to Marfa, Texas: Thursday October 27, 2011; 31 miles – Total so Far: 1,770 miles

At 9:00 A.M., Chano, who was born and raised in Sanderson, arrived at the motel. We loaded the bikes and gear. We said goodbye to our very helpful friend Danny who said he would follow us on Crazy Guy. On the way out of town, we stopped at a local gas station and food stop where I filled up Chano's truck and bought us all breakfast. As we drove to Alpine, the weather turned for the worse. It started to rain. The wind was a strong header as one of the first cold fronts was blowing in. "Not a good day for biking," I said. We passed a fully-loaded bicyclist headed our way. *What a brutal ride,* I thought.

I was glad not to be biking, but then again I really missed it and am always up for a challenge. Eventually riding in the truck was just too comfortable. I wanted to be outside in this "glorious" weather. Chano kept us company with stories about his trucking days. Jocelyn and I were not very good listeners, as we were frequently napping while Chano kept talking. Bikers on a trip can nap anywhere!

We made good time with the 83 miles to Alpine and quickly found the bike shop before 11:00 A.M. Chano was another nice guy on the road as he hung around to make sure we could get back on the road.

Fortunately, Bikeman was open although he usually does close on Fridays. We were warmly greeted by John who said I needed a new chain and rear gear cluster. He replaced both and I went on a test drive. The Beast was shifting okay but still not as smooth as I would have liked. He did adjust the derailleurs and said they were pretty worn but that they should make it to California. John did say that on a cross-country trip, bicycle chains should be replaced at least every 2000 miles because they tend to stretch. He measured the Surly's chain and said it was good for another 500 miles or so, but since he had a good chain in stock, we had it replaced. On my next cross-country trip, I promised myself that I would pack a spare chain, after having mine get twisted like it did in the middle of nowhere. If the chain doesn't work, you are stranded.

As we said goodbye to John, he asked, "Are you riding halfway back to Sanderson to make up those miles?" He said that with a smile.

I replied, "No, we are not purists."

He laughed. "I wouldn't either, especially on a day like this," he said. "You will ride plenty of extra miles to make those up."

We found the lunch spot he had suggested. Since it was cold and windy, I settled for a big bowl of broccoli soup and Jocelyn had a good toasted sandwich. When we were walking out, we met a biking couple heading south from Canada. We talked with them for a bit before hopping back on our bikes and finding a thrift shop. Jocelyn was getting cold, so she purchased a sweatshirt and a jacket for a few dollars. Now we needed full-fingered gloves since our regular biking gloves were not warm enough. A local hardware store had just what we needed. A local thermometer read 37 degrees, so I guess we *were* cold! We headed out of town on the road to Marfa with a brisk headwind. After a few miles, I was confused by the road signs and GPS since they didn't seem to match.

There were two border patrol agents on the roadside, so I asked them if this was the road to Marfa and they said yes. This was another case of being confused by the GPS, as the road number actually changed but didn't register with the GPS.

The ride was very pretty as it curved around a low mountain. As we curved even more and started descending, the wind became our friend and we quickly arrived in Marfa, Texas after a fast 31 miles. There was a campground on the outskirts of town, but we both shook our heads and said no way in this cold. When you've gotten used to the "motel lifestyle", camping in 30-degree weather doesn't sound too appealing. We found the Thunderbird Hotel on the other side of town, and since the daily rate was higher than any other place we had stayed in, we negotiated for a lower rate. Throughout this trip we had found that motel rates are very negotiable. We have even scored "bicycle rates"! The room was really clean and "artsy", so we checked in and enjoyed it. John from Bikeman had told us to dine at Padres, a local bar and grill. We thoroughly enjoyed a few hours while watching the World Series with the locals and savoring the local brews. I knew we had a big ride ahead of us tomorrow, so we left and had a good night's sleep.

"Dad is so slow — I guess I'll have a siesta"

Day 33: A Long, Cold, Windy Ride to Van Horn, Texas
Friday October 28, 2011; 76 miles – Total so Far: 1,846 miles

We were lazy in the morning as it was very cold out. We put off riding until the sun was spreading more warmth, had a good breakfast at the Thunderbird Hotel, and then packed and waited. Packing and loading had finally gotten easier, and we were very efficient at only unpacking the minimum. We had finally organized everything into one pannier that we anticipated needing each night. We would just open up that pannier and remove those items so then all the panniers could be left on the bikes.

We finally left at 9:30 A.M. because we were tired of sitting around. Jocelyn wore a face cover and looked as though she was ready to rob a bank in the Old West! At the start the headwinds were light, but they steadily grew. As we left Marfa, we passed a sign that read, 'No services for 74 miles'. I said to Jocelyn, "It will be a long day if the wind picks up more," but we made the commitment and rode on.

The road and shoulder were both very rocky with low-cost chip-seal. I tried to ride the shoulder line as it was smoother on the thick white paint. The traffic was light, and the miles disappeared behind us. We made good time up until the small and no-services town of Valentine, Texas. On the way out of the one-horse town, we saw some fellow bikers heading east. We were greeted with the words, "This must be the father and daughter adventure!" Dave and Jo from England had been following our adventure on Crazy Guy as they were making their own! How cool was that to meet fellow Crazy Guy bikers! They were on a tandem and traveling from San Diego, California to Orlando, Florida. Like us, they were somewhat following the ACA southern route. We had a nice talk with them and compared notes. Dave said there had been snow on the Van Horn foothills when they left and also to be careful of several loose dogs right outside of town. We, in turn, gave them a rundown on Marfa. When we parted ways, Dave said, "I would wish you fair winds, but we want them!" He got *his* wish.

As we rode out of Valentine, the wind came up very strong and cold. We struggled to make headway, but it was very slow going. The scenery was a good diversion, as there were wide expanses of ranches containing horses, cows, and bulls. We were also having a look at our first mountain ranges. I'm sure that some would say, "You ain't seen mountains yet," but coming from Florida, these were mountains to us. We passed a very impressive several hundred acre pecan tree farm and saw I-10 and Van Horn about 15 miles out. They appeared so close, yet they were so far away in a very strong headwind. We pushed as hard as we could, but it still took us over two hours before we rode into town. This was one of the hardest "end of the day" rides we had been on yet. We found the Best Western that Dave and Jo had recommended and checked in. It was getting late, so we cleaned up, walked to a nearby restaurant, and sat at the bar for dinner. While we were eating and watching the World Series, three guys came in and sat next to us. We overheard them talking about Kennedy Space Center, so I told them that I had worked there. They had been laid off like I had been, but they had been hired on with a local space company working on a commercial launch endeavor. It certainly is a small world. We both quickly grew tired and returned to the motel for laundry duty and web site updates. Tomorrow, we would head west and try to make it out of Texas.

Riding a lonely Texas road on the way to Van Horn

Day 34: We Tried to Make it to El Paso, but The Beast Broke Again
Saturday October 29, 2011; 99 miles – Total so Far: 1,945 miles

We were on the road in the early-morning cold, as our goal was El Paso at a distant 120 miles. We chose to travel on the I-10 shoulder, as our research showed that it is a good, wide shoulder for bikers, and it is legal for bikes until you get to El Paso. Also, there are unappealing rocky side roads that parallel I-10. The beginning of the trip was quite spectacular as we rode through mountainous canyons. We spotted several other touring bikes headed east. The Beast was having problems while shifting my chainwheel to 3rd gear (the largest). The chain finally dropped as it broke through the plastic chain guard. *Here we go again with another jam,* I thought. This time I was able to remove the chain from the jam without it becoming twisted, but as I continued to ride and shift, the chain kept going over 3rd gear. The adjustment to keep the chain from doing this wasn't working; in fact, the chain would not move into gear when I shifted. The derailleur wasn't working at all, and, as a result, I could not shift to pick up speed on the downgrades. I could only spin the pedals so fast and then pause before slowing down and peddling again. After a few miles, this got very old until I came up with the idea to stop The Beast, get off, and physically move the chain onto the three gears of the chainwheel. By manipulating the chain this way, I was able to climb and then pick up speed on the downhills and flats. It was a very tiring effort but it worked, although it wasn't very safe with all the stopping on the I-10 shoulder.

We were finally able to make up some time and stopped for a delicious Mexican lunch at Angie's Diner in Fort Hancock. At this point, we were riding against the clock again as the sun was quickly setting. At sunset we rode into Clint, Texas after a 99-mile and often frustrating day and quickly found a nice motel. I worked on the plastic chain guard and was able to zip-tie it in place. Since the chain adjustment wouldn't work, maybe I could shift to 3rd gear without the chain going over. It seemed to work in the parking lot. We had a quick dinner, and then I called a fellow Crazy Guy, Joseph from El Paso, with whom I had been corresponding. He had offered to guide us through El Paso on the way to New Mexico. After looking at the GPS and maps, we welcomed Joseph's help. We would finally get out of Texas tomorrow!

Jocelyn: We went 99 miles today! Just shy of the big 100! Maybe I'll go ride a mile in the parking lot to just say I did a hundred miles in a day! This cold front has really been rather chilly for us. We were not prepared for it at all, and I have been covering myself completely to try and stay warm. Missing the Sunshine State! Tomorrow we will finally be leaving the Great State of Texas. It has been my favorite state because of all the culture, pride, and hills we have encountered, and with rather friendly drivers, too! I did have an emotional breakdown about three days ago and have overcome it, just like both my father and I have overcome the not at all flatlands like we're used to in Central Florida! Tomorrow, New Mexico!

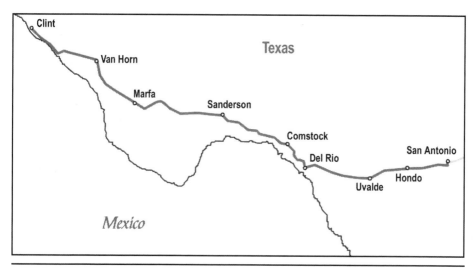

Day 27-Day 34: San Antonio, Texas to Clint, Texas

Chapter 11:
A Dash across New Mexico

Day 35: We're Out of Texas and in
Las Cruces, New Mexico
Sunday October 30, 2011; 86 miles –
Total so Far: 2,031 miles

We left Clint, Texas early on a beautiful, sunny, but cool morning. Traffic on I-10 was steadily picking up, but we didn't have far to the El Paso 375 Loop which, according to Joseph, would take us around the north part of town. There was more traffic on the loop, but we were soon on a nice bike path outside Fort Bliss Military Reservation and El Paso International Airport. Our goal was to find Joseph on the other side of the Anthony Gap, and from there he would ride with us into Las Cruces. Somehow we did manage to get lost, so I called Joseph and told him our cross streets. He found our location on Google and gave us more directions to Anthony Gap. I think the GPS was lost too, as we were lost once again through this confusing area. I couldn't get hold of Joseph, so we continued riding in the same direction. We stopped at an intersection and saw a jogger headed our way. He told us to keep going and we would soon see a sign for Anthony Gap. We continued on and soon we were in New Mexico! After the obligatory state sign pictures, we came to an intersection with Anthony Gap to the left. It had already been a long day and we weren't even halfway done.

Jocelyn yelled out at me, "I'll see you on the other side, Dad." I guess after all the time we had spent trying to find our way, she was ready to ride. She was soon out of sight as I slowly rode through the gap. The shifting sort of worked, but The Beast was still struggling. I longed for a smooth-climbing machine. The Anthony Gap splits the Franklin Mountains and is a very beautiful ride. The top was soon reached, and I coasted down the other side to see Jocelyn at the bottom, waiting for me as usual. And true to his word, there was Joseph. We found a place for lunch, and I called our friends Larry and Beth who had recently moved to Las Cruces from Cocoa Beach. The three of us then started on a beautiful Hwy 28 ride north to Las Cruces. The sun was going down fast, so we pushed on. We passed through many animal and crop farms and even passed over the bone-dry Rio Grande River. It was such a beautiful ride through cotton and alfalfa fields, horse farms, and eight miles of pecan trees. This pecan farm was the second largest in the world after a farm in Australia. Joseph had a wealth of information and discussed the history of the area as we rode side by side. There were no shoulders, but all the drivers were very courteous.

We soon found ourselves on the southwest side of Las Cruces, New Mexico and called Larry for directions. Jocelyn entered their address on her phone and read that we were 13 miles away. Joseph knew the Las Cruces bike path system, so we rode through New Mexico State University and found a bike path to take us across town. By this time it was dark, so we stopped and put our lights on. I do not like riding at night, so the combination of that and all the hills really took a toll on me. My left side started hurting again, and The Beast was not cooperating as my chain dropped a few times. Joseph, along with Jocelyn's phone, kept us on track. Joseph's chain dropped too, so it wasn't just me. Negotiating the increasing traffic at night was also stressful.

We finally pulled into Larry and Beth's house around 9:00 P.M., which is way too late to just show up at a friend's house with only a few hours' notice. But Larry and Beth greeted us very warmly with beer and a late dinner. Joseph even stayed and talked for a few hours before getting on his bike and heading back to El Paso — another 2 1/2 hours for him. He loves riding at night though and is well lit up. We wouldn't have found their house without him. Joseph is another one of those special people you meet on the road. Larry and Beth immediately made us feel at home, so I asked if we could spend an extra night as we were beat from the last few days. We declared another break day!

New Mexico — on the back route to Las Cruces

Monday October 31, 2011

Jocelyn and I both slept in and enjoyed some laziness. Larry was at work and Beth prepared us a fresh fruit and yogurt breakfast. She then went out for a few hours while we did laundry and updated our websites. This was a real treat as we hadn't had a day off in nine days. We browsed the maps and Internet to plan our next day. The ACA route goes north into the New Mexico mountains and then west into the Arizona mountains. But because of the balky Beast and my broken rib, we decided to stay south on I-10 into Arizona and then take I-8 to California. Taking I-10 is the easy way, and it is legal except for major cities like Tucson. We had family friends in Tucson and hoped to connect with them.

When Beth returned, she drove us to the path to get out of town to I-10. It seemed fairly rideable except for some steep hills and traffic. I figured it would take us a few hours to get there. It wasn't that far, but the traffic really concerned me because it would be during the morning rush hour. We had ridden through a few of those, and it was not fun.

We then drove to an excellent Mexican restaurant in the small, beautiful town of Mesilla, New Mexico. After that we went to — where else? — Walmart, for a few supplies. In retrospect, I should have taken The Beast in for an evaluation. Many people from the Crazy Guy site were urging me to get a new bike. Jocelyn was really pushing me on that too, but I had put all my faith in The Beast, so I didn't do anything even though I had the time. Since it was Halloween, Beth bought more candy as she thought it might be a busy night. When we returned, Larry had purchased some beautiful steaks for grilling. Soon, we sat down for our best meal yet: steak, potatoes, and mushrooms. It was excellent and so was munching on candy as the trick-or-treaters flowed down the street. Larry and Beth eventually ran out of candy and turned off the porch light, but the kids kept coming. After an excellent and restful day, we were soon asleep and dreaming of the road.

Jocelyn: A much needed rest day for us today. After riding long distances for the past nine days, we have stopped in Las Cruses, New Mexico to visit with friends that just moved here from Cocoa Beach, Florida. Beth and Larry's house is another oasis for us, along with their cute little bird too!

Day 36: A Flat Ride to Deming, New Mexico through Scenic Vistas and More Headwinds
Tuesday November 1, 2011; 65 miles – Total so Far: 2,096 miles

I was up early repacking and checking over the bikes. Jocelyn slept in while Beth put together another fresh fruit breakfast with peanut-butter-topped English muffins. This was a great breakfast for riders. I decided it would be best to take up Beth's offer to take us out of town as I didn't want to deal with the cross town traffic. I removed all the panniers (since it was getting so easy by now), removed my front wheel, and loaded all except Jocelyn's bike into Beth's van. As Beth and I drove the 20 minutes to I-10, I was pleased with my decision as the traffic was heavy. She dropped me off on a side road and returned for Jocelyn and her Surly. As I was putting my bike back together, an older couple riding by stopped and asked if I was okay as I had all the panniers scattered around. It was a pleasure to talk with these long-time bikers from Las Cruces. They said they had always wanted to ride cross country but being caregivers for both of their parents took most of their life. Now in their mid-80s, they didn't think they were strong enough even though they ride almost every day. Beth and Jocelyn soon drove up and talked with them too. They were such great people for their parents, but they now realized that age had caught up to them. I encouraged them to follow their dreams and maybe have a support vehicle follow them, or maybe they could join a tour group. They said they would look into that and were encouraged after seeing Jocelyn and I riding.

We all said our goodbyes, and Beth said to give her a call if we had any problems down the road. She said that she would gladly drive out and assist us. We said our thanks to both Larry and Beth for such a nice visit. We rode up the I-10 on-ramp and were quickly on our way to Deming. It was only 65 miles, so I thought that it should be an easy day. I would be eating my words by sundown.

We hadn't been on such a flat road for a few weeks, so we sped along with a small headwind. There are side roads that parallel I-10, but they were rough. Traffic was light and the shoulders were good, so we stayed on I-10. We occasionally passed a sign that read, 'Bicycles Stay on Shoulder' so we knew it was legal. We came upon a border patrol inspection station that was checking for illegals. We had passed through several of these. There were no bike lanes, so we just lined up with the cars. We were asked the standard two questions: "Where are you from?" and "Where are you going?" The border patrol officers were always very friendly and told us to "Stay safe." This one was no exception.

Since the headwinds were picking up, I tried to shift between gusts to pick up speed but The Beast wouldn't shift. I didn't feel like stopping and manually moving the chain, so our speed decreased considerably. Jocelyn took off on her speed runs, sometimes completely disappearing. Several trains were out, so that was a nice diversion. I caught up with Jocelyn at the tourist store in Akela Flats. We were both hungry so we went inside for a hot dog and soda. The store was a treasure trove of Old West trinkets, so we looked through all kinds of "interesting" stuff like rattlesnake heads, roadrunners, scorpions, and such. As we were getting ready to leave, a couple leaving at the same time asked where we were going. When we said, "San Diego," he said, "It must be tough to ride into such strong headwinds." I replied that it wasn't bad and that it had only been blowing around 15 mph or so. He laughed at that and said, "Good luck."

Needless to say, when we resumed our ride the wind was howling. The couple from the store rode by with a horse trailer and waved. It hadn't been blowing anywhere near this when we had stopped at the store. Jocelyn gave me that, 'You just ate your words, Dad!' look as we slowly pedaled westward. We both laughed and said, "Oh well!"

We had about 20 miles to go with an hour before sunset. This was going to be another painful ride at the end of the day. I counted each mile as it ticked away. Many billboards advertising motels started appearing, and we decided to stop at the first road in town. We finally made it to Deming at sunset and spotted a Holiday Inn across the street from a small food mart. I looked around inside and didn't see any beer, so I asked the clerk. He told me, "Follow the curve of the road for a mile."

Back on the bikes into the wind, we searched and searched but could not find another store. Since we were both frazzled, I decided that this would be a "No beer night", so we turned around and flew back to the Holiday Inn and claimed the last room! It was a 'smoking' room but we didn't care. This was one of the first motels we had stayed in that had a bar and restaurant inside. After a quick shower and laundry duty, we were seated at the bar, having a nice, cold draft beer. After a few beers, we each had a nice pasta dinner and then walked in the cold wind back to our room. As I lay down in bed, I could hear the wind howl and wondered if we were going to have to fight that in the morning.

Day 37: A Windy Slow Day and Then a Truck Ride to Lordsburg, New Mexico Wednesday November 2, 2011; 35 miles – Total so Far: 2,131 miles

It was a very cold and windy start for our ride to the next town of Lordsburg, as the wind had not let up at all during the night. As we headed west into the strong headwind, I looked into the mirror. Jocelyn had stopped and was waving to me. I turned around, thinking, *Not another flat!* Yes, it was her 5th flat on the trip (I hadn't even had one yet!). The wind howled and we were on the I-10 shoulder — not a good place to change out the tube. I looked off the shoulder, but it was nothing but gravel and thorns. The tube change out was quick as my hands were so cold. They shook as I pulled out two thorns from the Surly's front tire. I was very disappointed that these long thorns punctured the Schwalbe tires. Before we left, we examined all four tires and pulled out many more thorns that hadn't been completely imbedded yet. We had found during the trip that most of the thorns were concentrated around the towns. Thorns and tire wires are the bane of bikers.

As we continued west, the wind grew stronger and our speed decreased. After several hours we had only gained 35 miles, and at that point we were averaging around 5mph. It was mid-afternoon and we still had another 30 miles to go when we arrived at a full-service rest stop. Once there, we ate whatever we had packed away in the panniers and looked at our options. We calculated that it would take another 5-6 hours, around 8:00 P.M. before arriving in Lordsburg. We didn't want to be on I-10 after dark, so we decided to try and find a ride. Obviously, the ride would need to be a pickup or tractor trailer truck. The hunt was on.

I talked with a few truckers who said they would like to help us but were not allowed to pick up hitchhikers per company rules. All the pickups and large vans that stopped were full of stuff, so there was no room there. I had been watching one large tractor trailer for a while but hadn't seen anyone around it. Eventually I saw a Mexican truck driver walk around to the passenger side and try the door before walking back to the driver's side. I walked up to him and saw that he was trying to get the driver's door open. I said "Hi" and explained that my daughter and I were on bicycles and we were looking for a ride into Lordsburg. He looked at me and said, "Keys?" I didn't understand what he was saying, so he repeated, "Keys?" I finally figured out that he was trying to tell me his keys were locked inside the cab. He spoke very little English but wanted me to help him get inside. He worked a coat hanger on the side vent window while I pushed, and he eventually was able to reach around and unlock the door. The entire time, I was looking around and hoping that this was his truck. I expected someone to walk up and find me helping him break into this truck to steal it. I was very nervous about that. Once the door was open, he said, "Okay, we go."

At last — a ride!

I ran over to Jocelyn and said, "Let's go quick before he changes his mind."

When we got to his truck, he opened the trailer door and motioned for me to climb in. I climbed in and he and Jocelyn passed up both bikes which I laid down on the floor. As soon as the Surly was in, the door slammed shut! I immediately thought something bad was going to happen as I was in total darkness. He had just trapped me inside the trailer and Jocelyn was alone outside. I panicked as I thought about several gruesome scary movies I had seen. It seemed like forever before the door swung open and the driver latched it back. "The wind," he said.

I hopped down and Jocelyn yelled, "Dad, are you okay? You don't look too good."

"I'll tell you later," I replied.

We climbed up into the cab and the driver quickly motioned for Jocelyn to move back behind the seats. As he closed the curtains, he said, "The police can't see." And with that we took off.

During the next 30 miles we made scattered conversation. He gave us each a soda and talked about his trucking life. The miles quickly went by and he said he was going to Tucson if we wanted to continue with him. I politely declined and told him that we would ride our bikes. At the first exit into Lordsburg, he pulled over on the off-ramp and then up on the other side on-ramp before stopping and letting us out. I was going to pay him $20, but he quickly jumped back in the cab like he was scared that someone would see him. He turned out to be a really nice guy, but I think the door closing on me had taken away a few years!

He ended up dropping us off at a really good spot in Lordsburg, as there was a grocery store, a restaurant, and a motel right on the corner. Jocelyn swam in the motel pool as I did laundry, and then we had a nice dinner. What a day! I fell asleep dreaming of a nice boring ride tomorrow.

Shredded steel-belted tire — the bane of bicyclists. The wire pieces break off and scatter along the shoulder. They are very sharp and easily puncture the tire and tube.

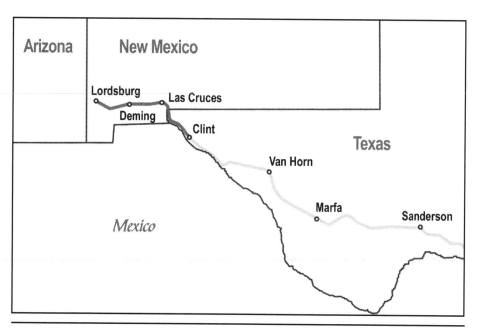

Day 35-Day 37: Clint, Texas to Lordsburg, New Mexico

Chapter 12:
Remote Navigating through Arizona

**Day 38: Today We Flew into Arizona –
After Jocelyn's 6th flat!
Thursday November 3, 2011; 76 miles –
Total so Far: 2207 miles**

Considering all the nursing I had been performing just to keep The Beast working, and also the continued ache in my left side, we decided to continue on I-10 into Arizona and Tucson. The northern ACA route involved too much climbing with those conditions. We realized that we were going to miss a beautiful part of the country, but we believed it just could not be done at this time.

We rode out of Lordsburg, New Mexico with a new cold front bringing 25 mph southeast cold winds that brought the wind chill down into the 20s. Fortunately the wind was on our quarter. A few miles out of town, we were stopped by Jocelyn's 6th flat. Because of the cold, it was a hard fix to pull out yet another wire. We were quickly on the road again with the wind blowing us toward Arizona. Several trains provided beautiful and dramatic views, especially through the Steins Mountain Pass into Arizona. After the celebratory pictures, we stopped at the first rest stop so I could call my family friends Howard and Carol in Tucson. They had been dear friends of my parents when they lived in Oxnard, California. I left a message and we continued into Arizona.

By now the wind was at our tail, and we made great time even though the shoulder was full of bumpy cracks. This was a little trying, but the tailwind brightened our spirits. We stopped at a gas station in Bowie for a quick sandwich and then got back on the road. Another time change gave us an extra hour, so we continued onto Wilcox, Arizona and looked at our options. The next town of Benson was about 35 more miles or maybe two hours away. It was about two hours until sunset, and I really liked the tailwind we had. About that time, Howard returned my call so I asked him about the road to Benson. He said it was pretty hilly with a few mountain passes and there was nothing between. We decided that it would be best to stay in Wilcox so that we would not be riding at night. Howard also told us that another front was coming down and to expect blustery weather for the next 24 hours. I told him that we would at least get into Benson the next day and then would see what the wind was doing.

I hesitate to invite ourselves into a friend's home without a given time, but that is the way of the biker. The weather and roads are always in control. We found a nice, inexpensive motel in Wilcox, did the laundry, and walked across the I-10 overpass to an excellent Mexican restaurant. Once in bed, I kept thinking of the tailwinds wasted by staying here and worrying about tomorrow's weather. It would turn out that I had good reason to be concerned.

We don't see this kind of scenery in Florida

Day 39: A Hard, Cold, and
Very Windy Ride to Tucson, Arizona
Friday November 4, 2011; 77 miles –
Total so Far: 2,284 miles

As we watched the morning news, we learned that a high wind advisory was set for 11:00 A.M. After a quick continental breakfast, we were on our way, hoping to make Benson before this advisory set in. There was a lot of climbing early on, and Jocelyn picked up her 7th flat of the trip. I don't know if you are counting, but that made it three mornings in a row! Needless to say, we, especially Jocelyn, were upset about this record. This time the culprit was a large screw imbedded in her rear tire. I started to say, "You should have seen this," but when I got that look, I shut up. I think she was mad at herself. By now we were experts at changing out the tube, so it was no big deal. It is more hassle at the end of the day because of the added patch chore. We rolled into Benson, Arizona and saw the high wind advisory flashing on an I-10 overpass sign. So far the wind had actually been in our favor, so we were good. We pulled over for lunch and again looked at our options. We looked at the steep climb out of Benson, and by looking at the GPS track we thought that the wind would continue to be our friend. Were we ever so wrong.

We called and talked with Carol and said that we were on our way. Once again there is nothing between Benson and Tucson, so it was a commitment. At 1:00 P.M. we started climbing and climbing just to get out of town. There was a major road construction project on I-10 that almost completely unnerved us. The shoulder was either a concrete barrier or full of debris. We fought with staying as close to the side as possible with the traffic trying to get around us. We had no business on I-10 with the sporadic shoulders, and I don't blame all the truckers and cars that honked at us, as we had unknowingly put ourselves in this precarious situation. This continued for mile after mile in tremendous headwinds and hilly terrain. There were several times I thought that for a touring biker it doesn't get any worse than this. We stopped often whenever we heard an odd tire noise. These noises turned out to be steel-belted radial tire wire pieces getting stuck in our tires. Each time we stopped, we pulled several wires out.

We finally worked our way out of the mountain passes and dropped down into Tucson. I answered my ringing phone, which I normally don't have on while riding, and it was Howard saying he could meet us on an off-ramp into Tucson instead of us trying to find their house. He had looked at the wind and figured we were probably having a pretty tough time, and was he ever right. We pulled off at one of the early exits and saw Howard and his truck waiting for us. We were so beat up that we just threw our bikes into the truck bed. It would have been several more confusing miles into a stiff headwind if Howard hadn't picked us up.

When we reached their home, we moved our bikes to their back porch and were shown the outside fridge with cold beer! Soon there were steaks and fish on the grill along with lots of stories about my mom and dad. It was a wonderful time to be with Howard and Carol, as they had been so close to my parents. Having just lost my dad, I grew very teary. Actually, we all did. It was a nice way to end a tough day and we quickly fell asleep in their comfortable home. We were also welcomed to stay longer, so Jocelyn and I agreed to a break day!

Saturday November 5, 2011:
Break Day in Tucson, Arizona

Howard prepared his delicious homemade pancake recipe while Carol volunteered at the local base thrift store. We spent a few hours studying various maps and discussing possible routes. They had an impressive selection of maps from all their years of traveling to California. Howard said there was a good side road parallel to I-10 that would take us into Casa Grande, and from there the best bet was to take I-8 to Yuma and then to California. Just hearing the word California got Jocelyn and I excited. We also started feeling a bit sad because the trip would be over soon. At least I was anyway. I think Jocelyn was eager to complete the ride so that she could get on with her future. She really missed home. I, on the other hand, was dreading my future. Cary and I were going to clean out my family home in Oxnard, California. There were 61 years of life to remove. It wasn't the labor I was dreading but the heartache.

Howard drove us to a popular bicycle shop to stock up on tube patches. I did have an assortment of peel-and-stick patches and also the glue on patches, but we found the peel-and-stick did not adhere well. We grabbed a handful of the glue on variety and also purchased two new pairs of socks. With daily use and laundry our original socks had worn quite thin, so this was a real treat — plus they looked cool!

After that, Howard took us to the home of some old family friends on Andee's side of the family. Pat and his wife Shannon live in a nice house overlooking a beautiful canyon where we sat outside and enjoyed lunch. After lunch we were driven back to Howard and Carol's home. Their son Jon, along with his wife Yvonne and son Zack, soon joined us. Jon and his wife are active in the Tucson biking community. He brought along his bike stand and tools and soon had The Beast on the stand for inspection. He cleaned, adjusted, and lubed the chain and cables. The derailleurs were very rough to operate but he got them working again and said The Beast should make it. Jon also put the Surly on the stand and gave it a quick cleaning and lube. I am amazed at how much dirtier my bike was. After all, we had been riding the same road!

That evening we had a huge and delicious pasta dinner. The stories and laughter flowed as we were drawn into their family. When they had lived in Oxnard, California, Jon and his sister had looked at my parents as grandparents. After dinner, Howard and I discussed the proposed route with Jon as he had ridden it before. With the exception of a few hills and then a mountain pass climb into Yuma, The Beast should do okay. We were soon dreaming of the road again. It's funny how you can take one day off but can't wait to get going again.

Jocelyn: We are in Tucson Arizona! Made it into Arizona yesterday and have been battling very strange strong winds. The gusts were up to 35 mph in some canyons today, and also the wind kept going from headwinds to our side and then to tailwinds! Semi-trucks would speed past us, and I really felt a part of a vacuum force being sucked in! Scary, but all around so beautiful! Beautiful rock formations, mountains, and cactus sightings! We're staying at a family friend's home tonight and tomorrow night. Tomorrow we are going to be tourists and check out Tucson. We are getting close to being on the long road, Hwy I-8. It was closed in some parts because of the high winds and dust storms!

Day 40: A Pleasant Ride from Tucson to Casa Grande, Arizona – with the Exception of One Small Detail Sunday November 6, 2011; 63 miles – Total so Far: 2,347 miles

After another delicious breakfast, Howard and Carol drove us to the side road that parallels I-10. From there we unloaded our bikes and said goodbye. Tucson is a very beautiful and biker-friendly city, and our friends really made us feel welcome. We said our thanks to Howard and Carol and pedaled on.

Since it was Sunday, there were several packs of roadies speeding by. Occasionally the pack would slow down and talk with us about our trip. They all seemed jealous that we were living this adventure. They would then hit their afterburners and soon be out of sight! We passed a local landmark, Picacho Peak, on a sunny, windless day. Several miles later, I felt my rear tire sliding back and forth and thought, *This is strange.* I soon came to a halt with my first flat tire! I could not believe it. I had almost crossed the country without a flat. Jocelyn just laughed and kept saying, "Ha Ha!" It served me right after the way I had teased her. I found several wire pieces stuck in the tire with only one actually penetrating the rubber. After a quick tube replacement we were on our way. We stopped at a few food marts with air stations but could not find one that worked. So I just pumped it up as well as I could and continued on the road. The score was 7-1 now!

We came to a confusing part of the side road, but I remembered Howard and Jon giving me specific instructions to get through this area.

As we pedaled into the small town of Eloy, we stopped at an Italian restaurant and split a pizza. A few miles later we found a nice motel in Casa Grande. This was a good spot, as I-8 was a block away, plus there was Eva's Fine Mexican Food right across the street. We checked in and were soon enjoying Dos Equis Amber and tacos. Next up would be Gila Bend, Arizona.

My one and only flat on the entire trip

Monday November 7, 2011: Delayed by a Cold Front

The sound of thunder woke me up several times during the night. I was up at 6:00 A.M. for good when the rain started. It looked like another front was coming through. As I watched the lightning, Jocelyn woke up and I said, "Go back to bed. We may not be going anywhere today." According to the television news, this new front wasn't going to pass until early afternoon. It is 65 miles to Gila Bend, so we scrubbed for the day. I did a little research on the Internet and found that there was a movie theater in downtown Casa Grande. After being lazy all morning, we called a cab and were off. The theater was in an outside mall and we were freezing in our shorts. We watched a movie, had lunch, and then walked around the mall until we were too cold, and then we took a cab back to the motel. It was an expensive day as the round trip cab fare was $35. This was for a total of 14 miles! Since they were the only service in town, the price was high. The one bonus of staying the extra day was another dinner at Eva's! We retired early with thoughts of sparse desert riding to Gila Bend.

Day 41: A Nice Ride through the Deserted Desert
Tuesday November 8, 2011; 65 miles –
Total so Far: 2,412 miles

We were on the road at sunrise and had an easy ride up the I-8 on-ramp, and then we continued around the Casa Grande Mountains. It was a fun ride through the low mountain pass into a large agricultural farming area. The traffic was light and the shoulder was mostly smooth and clean. We continued through another small mountain pass and dropped down to Sonoran Desert National Monument. We stopped many times to take pictures of the wide assortment of cacti. This was all fascinating to us beach people. The cold front from the day before gave us northeast winds, so the ride was easy. In this part of the country, cold fronts are usually followed by a day and a half of strong northeast winds before becoming westerly again. We found this out quickly and learned to take advantage of these wonderful tailwinds.

It seemed like only a few hours later we were in Gila Bend, Arizona. We stopped at the first food mart for a quick sandwich and to look at our options. It was early afternoon, so there was plenty of riding time available and we wanted to take advantage of the tailwinds. But per the GPS, the nearest campground was 70 miles away in Mohawk Valley, and Yuma was around 110 miles away. The GPS didn't show any motels between Gila

Bend and Yuma. Both sides of I-8 have wire fencing to keep cattle off the interstate, so stealth camping wouldn't be so stealthy. Reluctantly, we decided to get a room in Gila Bend.

Gila Bend was the hardest place so far to find a vacancy. We went from one motel to another, but they were all booked due to a large solar power plant being constructed outside of town. Only one other time had we had problems getting a room, and that was in Texas on a Saturday night. The solar power plant construction workers in the Gila Bend area had been living in the motels for several months.

We finally found your classic "old flea bag" motel that had one room left. It was our dumpiest place yet. The bed sheets were hung all around the green pool fencing to dry. Once inside the room, Jocelyn got on her bed and started pulling off all the hairs. I did the same thing. In most motels, we immediately remove the bedspreads and place them on the floor. It is amazing that we never encountered any bedbugs. We did take several precautions though. From all the laundry we did and our panniers full of stuff, we had expected to pick up something, but fortunately that never happened. In this room we were very cautious where clothes and laundry were placed. Needless to say, the bathroom was disgusting. Neither of us used the shower and I didn't shave as the water was cold. The washing machines placed outdoors next to the pool drained onto the parking lot and didn't complete the spin cycle. The drying took over an hour. I stood outside and drank beer while doing the laundry, as I didn't trust anybody here. I did talk to some workers who had lived here for several months and thought this was a great place because the company was paying for their rooms. That afternoon I saw several first shifters arriving with their arms full of beer. What a life! For dinner, we unfortunately chose a Burger King across the street as it was too cold to walk further. We planned for an early start as Yuma was over 100 miles away and we wanted to take advantage of the continuing tailwinds. I figured we should have that advantage until noon or so.

Some shoulders are a little rough

Day 42: "7:10 to Yuma!"
Wednesday November 9, 2011; 107 miles –
Total so Far: 2,519 miles

We boarded our bikes at 7:10 A.M. for the ride to Yuma! We were surprised at all the farmland instead of desert. The farmland then turned into a huge solar power plant construction project that went on for several miles. The tailwind was still with us although it was dying down, so we continued to push it. Jocelyn would ride ahead, and then I would power up to her. Then she would pull away. There was hardly any traffic, and once again I pretended I was on a horse and trying to get away from the bad guys. I listened to Cary's "Glorious music" with a Western theme and I rode hard. This is what riding is all about.

There was nothing but empty road through the desert. This continued for many miles until I saw that Jocelyn had pulled over, and my first thought was, *Flat tire number 8*, but she had stopped at a town sign she didn't want me to miss. It said 'This Exit, Sentinel Arizona, Historic Sites, Middle of Nowhere, Gas-Food-Diesel'.

I liked the 'Middle of Nowhere' part because it was true. In fact, we passed Sentinel School with grades K-12. What a small town.

We passed by the town of Dateland which is really full of date trees and their famous date shakes, but we decided not to stop as we had a lot of desert to cover. Our first mountain pass for the day was through the Mohawk Mountains. There were several more beautiful mountain ranges and passes ahead. An occasional train would appear with a mountain backdrop. Needless to say, this was one of my favorite rides. We stopped at a food mart in Tacna, Arizona after making good time for 74 miles. Also in Tacna was a motel that didn't register on our GPS. At the speed we were going the day before, we could have made it. There was a campground here too. It was only five hours since we left Gila Bend. I was impressed, as 15 mph is really good for us. As we ate lunch I watched a flag flip to the other side. The northeast winds were now out of the northwest and coming on strong. For a fleeting moment I thought about the motel and campground, as we had 75 miles for the day. But then I looked at the place and thought we just had a rest day, so we continued.

We powered into the increasing headwinds. The beauty of the surrounding mountains kept me going. We came up to Telegraph Pass of the Fortuna Foothills in a very heavy wind and began our climb. The Beast was fighting my shifting and dropped the chain again. I got off and manually shifted the chain but was unable to pedal due to the steep pass. Jocelyn was way ahead somewhere and I started walking. I walked until I got to the top where I was able to pedal again. I coasted down, as I couldn't shift either gear. Jocelyn was waiting on the other side. We continued on into the strong wind without being able to shift. I nursed The Beast to Yuma and found a Holiday Inn off the first off-ramp. It was past sunset so we settled down after our longest day yet. Dinner found us next door at Pizza Hut and then to bed exhausted. With mixed emotions I thought of California and fell asleep.

Jocelyn: We made it to Yuma, Arizona! 107 miles — wow! That makes the farthest miles we have done in one day and I am so proud of my dad and I. We kicked butt for 7 hrs and 38 minutes across the desert and a mountain pass! We are stoked for tomorrow, as we will be crossing the border into California. This has been one amazing journey!

A typical motel room.

An early-morning ride

Day 38-Day 42: Lordsburg, New Mexico to Yuma, Arizona

Chapter 13:
A Bumpy Entry into California

Day 43: "California, Here We Are!"
Thursday November 10, 2011; 77 miles –
Total so Far: 2,596 miles

We left the Holiday Inn early and found Hwy 95 South. This bypass of I-8 took us to the west end of Yuma. It was a nice morning to ride through Yuma's agricultural region, and it reminded me of my hometown of Oxnard, California which is also (or used to be) a major agricultural area of Southern California. The shoulders were pretty bumpy and dirty due to tractor use, but the traffic was light so we moved onto the road. After several miles we were on the northwest side of Yuma and once again entered I-8. Traffic was heavy for rush hour but the shoulders clean and wide. There was a side road alternative, but it didn't seem like it would save us much as we would eventually need to return to I-8. We soon crossed the Colorado River into California, and what a banner moment it was as we had crossed the country on bicycles. We stopped and took several celebratory pictures on the side of I-8 with many drivers giving us good honks. As we were swinging around on the last big overpass, The Beast dropped the chain again. Since the traffic was heavy I tried to quickly get back on the road, but it took some doing as the rear derailleur pulley was broken and the chain was twisted again. I was able to get it set up in a single speed mode and we rode on. There was a 'Welcome To California' sign after the first 'California State Line' sign, so we stopped at that one too for more pictures. We had arrived, so we seized the moment!

We rode through the California Agricultural Inspection Station without being searched for fruit. We did have a few apples saved from breakfast that I had forgotten about. The increasing headwinds and hilly terrain was a bit difficult without being able to shift. I was tired of stopping and manually moving the chain, so I just plowed along. At this point I figured I could walk The Beast to San Diego if need be, as we were 10 days ahead of schedule. Andee and Cary were due to arrive in San Diego on the 20th, and we were not going to do the celebratory wheel dip in the Pacific until then. The ride by the Imperial Sand Dunes was amazing. The sand dunes are located on the southeast corner of California and are the largest mass of sand dunes in the state. The dune system extends north and south for more than 40 miles and is about five miles wide where we passed. As we continued on I-8, there were signs stating that bicycles are not allowed on California freeways. Since we didn't see an alternative, we continued on until a California Highway Patrolman stopped us near an off-ramp.

He directed us to go up the nearby on-ramp and move north onto old Evan Hewes Highway and that would take us to El Centro, our goal for the day. I am all for alternatives to get off the main road, so we were happy to oblige until we saw the conditions. The Evan Hewes Highway was all broken up with deep, wide ruts and sand. In fact, there were several road closed signs that stretched across the width. We were soon tired of this jostling road, and we were moving less than 5 mph. Jocelyn was really upset and didn't want to go any further. I didn't either but what was the alternative? We were directly parallel and could see I-8. As we bounced along, we saw the patrol car at the next three I-8 on-ramps. The Highway Patrolman was checking to see if we would attempt to reenter I-8. The thought of reentering had crossed our minds, but we didn't want to be arrested and the patrolman had said that we would be. It is the law, so we had to deal with it. Jocelyn wanted to try and find someone to pick us up, but none of the ramps were marked so we had nothing to go on. The ACA route is further north, but there was no way to get there at this point.

Jocelyn and I had crossed the country and gone through many hardships. We'd had our ups and downs, and we were being tested again. So we took a time out. She started walking her Surly and I rode The Beast. I soon lost sight of her, so I pulled over to walk and think. I think Jocelyn was ready for the ride to be over and being on this road was like the last straw for her. On the other hand, I wasn't ready for the trip to end and looked at this as a challenge to learn off-road touring. As I was walking through the desert, I saw her still walking her Surly and waited for her to catch up with me. I told her that according to my map we had about 20 more miles of this before the conditions would improve. The sun would set in five hours and we needed to go. At that point, we were both ready to move again so we pushed on by riding some, cursing some, and then walking some. We were both quiet and tired because of the day-in and day-out riding routine, and the strong headwinds on this day didn't help us.

After four hours of bouncing along the rutted highway, we split off on Hwy 80 East to the town of Holtville. Lunch was a quick sandwich and drink, and then it was a real push to find El Centro before dark. We had gained an hour when we crossed into California, and this saved us from riding in the dark. We rode through El Centro, and the GPS guided us to a very comfortable Holiday Inn on the west side of town. We had just completed one of our most mentally trying days, and since we are so far ahead of schedule and a cold front was expected to drop through, we decided to take the next day off.

We made it across the country!

"California, here we are"

Friday November 11, 2012: Break Day in El Centro

The anticipated cold front that was to bring stormy weather to El Centro was stalled further north. The day was cold and windy, but it was rideable. At this point we were trying to figure out our next move. San Diego was on the other side of the Mountain Empire, which is the southeast corner of San Diego County. The town of Pine Valley, in the Cleveland National Forest, is near the peak with an elevation of 3,800 feet. The Beast's climbing days were over, so I would not attempt that climb. We needed to hitch a ride and bike down to San Diego. Our goal was my sister and brother-in-law's home in Pacific Beach. I called Jim and we talked about our options. He said that the front was stalled but due to come through the next day with heavy rain.

Since Jim didn't need to be at work until 10:00 A.M., he volunteered to pick us up and drop us off after the peak. At this point, we decided to meet him in Ocotillo, have him drive us to Pine Valley, and then let us ride in from there. It sounded like a good plan, even though I thought we were wimping out on the climb. I still think of that climb and wish we would have at least tried to make it. I could have walked The Beast up. This was probably my biggest regret of the ride — not trying. With that, we knew we would finish the next day.

With our plans set, we decided to have a last lunch outing and found a nice bar where we ate and had a few beers. We discussed our "Father and Daughter Adventure" to length and were both sad that it was ending, but it was time.

Reminiscing about our journey over a few
cold ones before our ride into San Diego

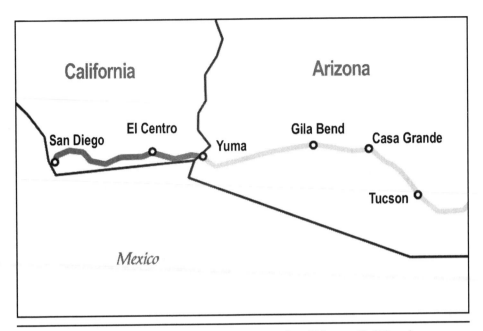

Day 43-Day 44: Yuma, Arizona to San Diego, California
(Pacific Beach on the ocean)

Chapter 14:
Wheel Stop in
Pacific Beach, San Diego

Day 44: We Arrive in Pacific Beach, San Diego, California During a Downpour
Saturday November 12, 2011; 41 miles –
Total for the Trip: 2,637 miles

We ate our last motel breakfast and were ready for the day. The 26 mile ride to Ocotillo was uneventful except for my chain dropping again. Jocelyn waited patiently while I wrestled the stuck chain out of the gears. Of course she was taking pictures of me, and I have far too many pictures of me working on The Beast. As we rode through Plaster City, the road became very bumpy with some parts worse than the ride two days earlier. We were back on the ACA route and soon in Ocotillo when Jim drove up with his truck. We loaded our bikes and then drove to Pine Valley. As we drove along, I couldn't help but think how disappointed I was not to be riding this beautiful climb with the rocky landscape. At this point, California does allow bicycles on some portions of I-8 as there is no alternative.

We stopped at In-ko-pah Park for a quick tour. This park has a large stone viewing tower along with a hike through a "boulder garden". Some of the boulders have animals carved out of them. After that, we drove through the approaching front and pouring rain to Pine Valley and had lunch at a local diner. Since the rain was not letting up, Jim said he would drive us until it did, as we didn't want to ride down the wet mountain road. We drove to Santee, and since the rain was slowing, Jim dropped us off on Mission Gorge Road and then left for work. As we got on our bikes, the downpour started again. We had all our rain gear and our lights on, so we proceeded to pedal through that mess.

The roads and especially the bike paths were flooded and crowded with Saturday traffic. We were totally drenched but loving it as we were sprayed by all the traffic, and we quickly found our way down Friars Road along the ACA route. The route then lead us to Sea World Drive and then Ingraham Street which we followed north to our Pacific Beach destination. We wanted to stop at a local bar, but since we were soaked we didn't think it wise to drip all over an establishment's floor. The local traffic seemed to know we were at the end of a big journey as there were lots of good honks. We were met in the pouring rain by my sister, Tish, and a banner made by Jim that he hung along the garage door. We had completed our adventure after 2,637 miles.

Jocelyn: We have done it! In 44 days we have bicycled across the country through various terrains, met many wonderful people, ate lots of tasty food, and survived our struggles. There were physical and mental setbacks and long, tiring 8-hour rides. After finally leaving Florida, we really flew down the roads while pushing our averages and challenging each other. What's next? Right now I plan to have a little rest and relaxation as we're going to be waiting for my mother and brother to fly west on the 20th. We all will be together for the ritual front tire dipping in the Pacific Ocean! My new favorite saying is "You Only Live Once" (YOLO).

Jim dropped us off in Santee, and then the rain started again.

Arriving at Tish and Jim's house in Pacific Beach

Sunday November 13, 2011 to
Saturday November 19, 2011

The night before, we celebrated the end of our journey with my cousin-in-law Claude and my niece Makani. Tish cooked a big pot of chili plus brought out a 21st birthday cake for Jocelyn. We were exhausted but stayed up late with tales from the road. Sunday morning I was up early to do my favorite activity in San Diego. There is a three mile walking, jogging, and bike path that runs along Pacific and Mission Beach from a little north of Crystal Pier south to Mission Bay Jetty. I really enjoy jogging that path and do so daily when visiting here. Even after 2,600 miles on my bicycle, today was no exception. During the next few mornings, Jocelyn joined me until we both were all of a sudden very sore. Since we hadn't run for several months, we were using parts of our legs that didn't get used while cycling. All of a sudden, running six miles really did us in. I was really surprised by that. Plus, we were walking everywhere as Jim and Tish were working. We ended up taking a few days off running and felt better. The following week we were back on the path with no pain.

We spent the next few days walking around town and enjoying the non-biking routine. One of Jocelyn's favorite things is tattoos, and I had been secretly thinking about a cycling one for my leg. I wanted something that would bond Jocelyn and me together forever. When I brought this up with her, she got excited about it too. We were thinking of a bicycle inside an outline of the United States. There was a time that I would never think of getting one, but this seemed like the right time in my life — so why not go for it. Jocelyn called her San Diego cousin, Makani, who has several tattoos herself, and found out where she goes on Garnet Avenue, Pacific Beach. As we walked there Tuesday morning, I saw a bike path sign with a very simple drawing of a bicycle.

"That's it, Jocelyn," I said. "Put that bike inside a U.S. outline map."

"Cool," she replied and took a picture.

We arrived at the shop and told the tattoo artist what we wanted. At first she thought it was a little strange, but once we told her about our journey she was really excited too. She used Jocelyn's phone to download the picture. Then she went to work on her computer and came out a few times with sample drawings. We changed this and added that until we were happy with the result. At that point Jocelyn could tell that I was getting worried about the procedure. The artist appeared again and said, "Ready?"

"My dad is first," Jocelyn said as she grabbed my arm. I soon had the outline taped on my left calf, and then I laid down on the table. At first it was somewhat painful, but I quickly got used to the needle running around my calf. As I lay there, I was hoping the bike was pointed to California and not Florida. I couldn't remember what the drawing looked like. When the tattoo was finished, that's the first thing I looked at and it was pointed to California. I lasted about a minute watching Jocelyn get tattooed. When a little blood came out, I went into the waiting room. We soon walked out of the tattoo parlor as "twins" with a big, white patch over the tattoo. On the sidewalk while waiting for the walk signal, a man asked us what had happened to have both of us injured in the same place. "Matching tattoos!" we said. At that he shook his head and walked off.

After that we found a nice fish restaurant and settled down with beer and fish. It was a fun two days just being lazy. I'm sure The Beast and the Surly felt neglected as we hadn't looked at them since Saturday.

Jim was off the next two days, so he played tour guide. Wednesday was spent as a lazy day slowly walking through the San Diego Zoo. Jim has an annual pass and comes here often and knows the best way to see everything, so we followed his lead. We had an excellent time exploring all the exhibits and animals. The patches were off our tattoos and we had several comments. "Excuse me, but did you just ride a bicycle cross country?" It not hard to figure out what our tattoo denoted! On Thursday we traveled to the California Maritime Museum in downtown San Diego. We went onboard the *Star of India* sailing ship, the replica of the HMS *Surprise*, used in the movie *Master and Commander*, the tall ship *Californian*, along with an American and Russian submarine and an old steam ferry. It was a great day for exploring these ships.

The following day we walked to a Pacific Beach restaurant and met a fellow Crazy Guy Dave for lunch. He had followed us on our trip and emailed several comments along the way, so it was nice to meet him. He and his wife have done many bicycle tours throughout the U.S. and were quite knowledgeable about touring bikes. We discussed several brands of possible tour or expedition bikes. The time flew by, and when Dave left, Jocelyn and I walked to the beach and came upon an outside beach bar where we sat in the warm sun and enjoyed a pitcher of Dos Equis Amber. We have been to very few places that have this on draft. On the way back to Tish and Jim's home, we stopped and checked out a few bike shops. It's fun to go into a bike shop while not having to think about fixing yours.

Soon it was Saturday. The next day Andee and Cary, along with her mom, Polly, and two of her brothers, Jeff and Greg, would meet us at Crystal Pier for our final ride to the Pacific Ocean.

Cape Canaveral, Florida to San Diego, California

Chapter 15:
Mission Complete

Final Ride: We Dip the Front Tires (and a lot more) in the Pacific Ocean! Sunday November 19, 2011

We loaded our bikes for the final time and moved them out of the garage. It was time for the last ride. I don't know why, but I was nervous as we rode down the street to the beach. We took our time to make sure everyone was there and confirmed that with a few phone calls. Jocelyn was very excited; I was too but more subdued. Part of me didn't want this to end. I had looked at an expedition bike in one of the shops and had told Jocelyn, "What if I get this bike and then we turn around and ride home to Florida?"

She excitedly replied, "Let's do it, Dad!"

If I wasn't planning on cleaning out my parents' home and didn't have a job prospect, I think we would have. Reality was soon caving in on me. Andee and Cary had been taking care of the house and dogs for the last several months, so it also didn't seem fair to take off again. In fact, I never told Andee what I was thinking. She has been a wonderful wife, letting me go on this dream adventure while not asking for anything in return.

As we rode down Mission Bay Blvd, I thought of the father and son duo that I saw several months ago while on a training run in Florida. They had started from Huntington Beach, California and were on their final ride to dip their tires in the Atlantic Ocean. As they rode by me, the father looked back at me and said, "Almost there!" I didn't know about them at the time, but I saw them later in the news. So as we neared Crystal Pier, I finally saw somebody to say "Almost there!" to. What a great feeling! We turned the corner to the beach and there was my family. It was another great feeling to be together again. Andee and Cary had stretched a banner out, and we had lots of hugs with them and Andee's mom and brothers.

Since it was a Sunday morning, there were lots of people walking around applauding us. Tish kept yelling out about us and the miles we had gone. She was our cheerleader! There was even a policeman who had driven up on the wide boardwalk and said, "I've been trying to pull these guys (us) over for the last several miles, but they wouldn't stop!"

The sky was threatening rain and we had one more thing to do.

Pacific Beach sand is softer than Cape Canaveral's, and, boy was it tough to walk the bikes down to the water. As I struggled, Cary helped me. I hope there isn't any rule out there that you can't have any assistance on your final ride! We finally made it to the water, and since it was way out we walked more.

"Dad, that's far enough."

"No, Jocelyn, we need to go further."

So we kept going. Then, as a wave rushed in, we tried to move back. Needless to say, we and the bikes were baptized. It was all good so we laughed it off. I then took out a bottle of champagne, shook it up good, and then uncorked it to spray Jocelyn as she jumped for joy. What a wonderful moment, especially with people cheering on the beach. This was like our last hurrah.

I knew I was going to miss my time on the saddle, but I would especially miss my time with my daughter, Jocelyn. We had shared a very special time together; in fact, how many fathers can say they have spent some real quality time such as this with their daughters? There had been a lot of growing, learning, laughing, and of course, crying. I don't know who has cried more, but I do know I did my share.

With the beach festivities over, reality set in. We walked The Beast and the Surly to my dad's car for unloading and then rode the bikes to a local bike shop. We left the Surly with them to ship to Matt's Bicycle Center in Cocoa Beach. I rode The Beast for a final time to Tish and Jim's home. As I did, I kept looking around for Jocelyn but she wasn't with me. *It really is over*, I thought, and then I started to cry again. I already missed her.

I took my time going back as I knew this was my last ride on The Beast. Just for the heck of it, I fiddled with the shifting and The Beast immediately dropped the chain. I just laughed, set the chain, and continued. The Beast would not be sent home to Florida; instead, I planned to donate it to a local school fundraiser. The Beast had character and is still missed today.

We all met in a nice La Jolla restaurant with more family and friends for brunch. I had a good time but felt very subdued. I actually had a hard time talking about our adventure, so I pretty much left it at that. My dad was supposed to be here and I was going to ride The Beast to his home in Oxnard, but none of that was going to happen. I often wonder if he would still be alive if I had gone to see him instead of starting the ride. When I last spoke to him the night before we left, he was very insistent that Jocelyn and I get on our bikes and start our ride. Whenever I told him that I could fly out, he kept saying, "No." He told me to "Keep the wheels going round and round and I will be with you all the way." My mom, my dad, and my little sister Sue were with us all the way. During the journey, whenever we cycled by a church or cemetery from Cape Canaveral to San Diego, I crossed my heart and said, "God bless Mom, Dad, and Susie."

My brother Cary and my mom Andrea.
This was the same banner from our start in Cape Canaveral.

From the left: my Uncle Jeff, Auntie Tish,
Uncle Greg, brother Cary, and my Gramma Polly

A jump for joy in front of Crystal Pier, Pacific Beach, San Diego

Thanksgiving Week and Reflections of Our Adventure

The week started out with us emptying all our bike gear on the garage floor along with removing equipment from The Beast. I was going to donate my bike, as it was a fine setup as a single-speed beach cruiser. We then bought several boxes and packed everything to send home to Florida. This took a few days and lots of postage. Soon Thanksgiving Day arrived, and it was a blessing for us to be safely with family again. I was teary-eyed all day, missing my mom and dad. Andee and Jocelyn were leaving for Los Angeles after dinner with Jocelyn's cousin Heather, as they were flying out the next morning. When they left, the Father and Daughter Adventure was officially over. My biking partner for the last several months was gone. I felt so empty.

As I look back and reflect, I find that the riding was relatively easy but the three weeks of delays were heart wrenching. Riding while knowing my dad was probably in his final days was a tough decision that no one except my dad and I agreed on. Riding with that decision playing in my head daily was tearing me apart. But once I decided to store the bikes and fly out to see him, a peace came over me. As I napped on the flight to Los Angeles, I remember waking up for just a few minutes and looking out the window at a layer of clouds lit up by the bright moon. It almost seemed like I was looking at heaven in a way. It was very beautiful, and I remember going right back to sleep. While driving home from the airport with Jim, I remembered that image and realized that it might have been about the time my dad passed as we were a few hours out from Los Angeles. I have thought about that many times since.

When we returned from California to renew our trip, we were very anxious to get back on the road especially since we were still in Florida. Then, on the third day, I fell and broke a rib and immediately thought that maybe we were not destined for this adventure. The pain was intense, but my first thought was, *Okay, now deal with this*. One painful week later we were back on the road and camped that first night. My breathing was labored and short while going up bridges and hills, but that just made me push harder.

The daily ritual of riding every morning turned into relief and joy. When we went to bed each night, there was the anticipation of not only where we would go but more importantly who we would meet the next day. The route was never really planned until the night before, which brought some worry but mostly a big smile to my face. People were shocked when we told them this. It was incredulous to think that we could not plan more than one day at a time. This made it an exciting adventure and of course sometimes daunting as related in all the late sunset arrivals. We chose our own route and would not hesitate to ride most of it again. The only thing we might do differently is to plan for more camping since we had hauled over 25 pounds of camping gear across country and only camped three times.

The days started rolling by, and soon we were finally out of Florida. We built our climbing legs in East Texas Hill Country. There were some moments of. "Why are we doing this?" but those were quickly erased. Whenever I found myself slowing down or thinking about how hard it was, I just pushed harder. In West Texas, the hills turned into Canyon Country, along with more doubts that were quickly erased. Our highest ascent was at 5,144 feet. While a lot of bikers dread Texas, we actually embraced this beautiful state. It was wide open riding country that put smiles on our faces.

Headwinds, hills, canyons, and mountains build character. Along that line, so does bicycle grease. I don't think a day went by where we weren't streaked with some on our legs or faces. When my chain first started dropping or I was manually moving the chain onto the gears, I would try to use a disposable glove or paper towel to avoid the grease, but after a while I just used my bare hands. We laughed at all the grease smeared all over us. Once we passed Texas, the trip went by quickly. It was New Mexico for a few days and then a few in Arizona. California seemed like a flash. Of course we did cheat when Jim picked us up and drove us 70 miles over the mountain range from Ocotillo to Santee. The Beast wasn't going to make it, and walking it seemed foolish. What a rush of emotions as we rode our last miles and the climb to Tish and Jim's home — it was one last climb in the pouring rain. After all, climbing, wind, rain, and bicycle grease all build character.

Chapter 16:
Cleaning Out My Parents' Home

December 2011; It's On to Oxnard
for an Emotional Job and then
Another Adventure Home to Florida

My mom and dad built our Oxnard, California family home in 1950, and this is where my two sisters and I were raised. It was the only home we ever knew. My mom passed away in 2008, a month before their 61st wedding anniversary, and left my dad heartbroken for the next three years until he went to join her. He always said that she had opened the door for him and it was just a matter of time. As Cary and I drove my dad's car home to Oxnard, I thought of the agonizing task ahead. We were going to peel away 61 years of living in the house, layer after layer.

Whenever I go home to Oxnard, I run to the beach every morning. It is something that I have always enjoyed and continued to do so on this, my last trip home. The timing always worked out well, because I would leave before dawn and return home about the same time my mom and dad got up. Then it was breakfast for all of us. This time I continued the same routine, except it was just Cary and me for breakfast.

I had talked with Andee several times about how to clean out my family home. She told me to just start bringing things out and, "You will know what to do." Well, I did just that and brought things out one at a time and either put them in a box for Tish or me or put them on a table to figure out later. This worked and continued to do so for over three weeks. Thanks, Andee. It was one cupboard at a time, one item at a time. We went out and purchased many boxes, tape, and packing materials. As the boxes were filled and marked, there was always another empty. If I thought it was good for a donation, it went in the donation box or pile. My parents had been members of the St. Vincent De Paul Society of Oxnard. They'd worked in the local food kitchen and had given out food to the needy on a weekly basis. They helped out even when they were older and couldn't lift the food boxes anymore, so other members of the society had to convince them to step down. They loved helping others, so we gave away many of their household items. The society came one afternoon and picked up a garage full of their household goods. I'm sure they are happy seeing other people helped by their donations.

My dad was very much loved in the neighborhood. When neighbors would come by to see Cary and me, I would ask them if there was something they wanted. I invited them in and said to take what they wanted, as my dad would love for them to have it. Some people started crying and we gave them things. This included furniture too. Tish and I thought about an estate sale, but it wouldn't be like my dad to sell his stuff. And in this way he is still in the neighborhood.

My mom was a picture-taking fanatic and filled over 85 albums with pictures of our childhood and then our new families when we were married. She'd made several albums for each grandchild. She so cherished all these albums and even added typed captions to the pictures. What were we to do with all these albums? Cary and I bought the best and fastest scanner we could find locally, and Cary commenced to scan each page. It took us all of the three weeks we were there to complete this task. Today, my childhood, marriage, and kids are all scanned. What a wonderful gift from my mom. And thanks, Cary, for all the extra work.

We rented a dumpster from the city, as there was a lot of unusable goods and trash stuck everywhere in the yard, two sheds, and garage. This made it a lot easier to clear the house. When we finished one room, we went and dove right into the next. With this kind of project, you can't slow down. The work was very painful and brought tears whenever we would find something attached to a memory. My mom and dad left several notes scattered in the various boxes and cupboards. Many of them started like this: "If you are reading this, then we are gone and we are sorry for this mess that we left." None of it was a mess, as they were so well organized. They kept every post card, letter, and greeting card that they ever wrote each other or that we ever sent them. All the letters and cards that I ever wrote them from the time I left home and joined the navy to just this year were saved in marked boxes. Each year was rubber banded together. Every day we were amazed at what we would find.

Throughout the years, whenever I had gone home, I always looked for my dad's old Schwinn shop bicycle, because I had asked him to save it for me when he retired in 1987. I hadn't seen it at the house, so I figured he had thrown it away. When we were kids he used to ride us around the block in a box he had added on the rear. As we were cleaning out one of the sheds, there it was! He did save it for me, but since it was totally buried I never saw it. I wanted to keep it and send it home, so we went to UPS for a bike box. We had been going to this UPS store pretty regularly to send boxes home to Florida. I took the rusty old bike apart but couldn't get one of the pedals off, so I ended up taking it to a bike shop. As we wheeled it into the store, the owner just stared at it and was excited looking at all the original parts. He wondered what my plans were for it, and I told him I was going to strip the rusty paint down and install new wheels and tires. At that point he was shocked and said not to touch this pre-WWII Schwinn and that it was worth around $5,000! The last few days as I was taking it apart, I thought about just throwing it away because of the condition. The owner of the UPS store we had been using is a bicycle collector, and he confirmed everything the shop owner told me. The bike is now sitting in the same box in my garage. I will install new tubes eventually but will not sell it. It is a classic that I will ride around the neighborhood, as my dad's old bicycle has a lot of character.

When I was home in Oxnard for my dad's funeral, I had been contacted by a potential employer for work at a remote NASA tracking station in McMurdo, Antarctica.

McMurdo Station is an American Antarctic research center located on the southern tip of Ross Island, on the shore of McMurdo Sound in Antarctica.

This sounded like the adventurous job I was looking for. I had sent the company a resume before my lay off but didn't hear from them until my neighbor who worked at the Kennedy Space Center tracking station gave me a contact name and I sent him my resume. I was told that they have trouble filling this position due to the strict medical and psychological testing required for anyone who "winters over" at McMurdo. I was definitely interested in the job and was told to call back when Jocelyn and I were finished with the bike ride.

When we arrived in San Diego, I contacted the manager who had called me. I was soon emailed many confusing medical forms and lists of the requirements to get "Physically Qualified (PQd). I was totally overwhelmed and wondered how I would get all this work completed by early January 2012. Since my doctor was in Florida, I had to find one here and schedule a very detailed physical within two weeks.

In addition to all the cleaning out, sorting, and packing, I was on the phone going through the yellow pages and finally was scheduled for a physical at a local urgent care center. When I arrived for this and gave them all of the requirements, they were a bit confused and overwhelmed themselves and had to call many other medical facilities to schedule all this work. Needless to say, the push for time was not on my side, and it didn't help that we were also up against the Christmas Holidays. I spent several days running around the county for these tests.

A few days before Cary and I were to leave for Florida, I flew to Denver, Colorado for my psychological exam. That in itself was quite an adventure, and I flew back to Los Angeles the next night. Cary had dropped me off at the airport, spent the night with his grandmother, and returned to pick me up. We were leaving in a few days so the work pace quickened. I met with a real estate agent in Oxnard and signed the paperwork to sell our family home. It was a sad time, but neither Tish nor I wanted to keep the house. We had our own homes in San Diego and Cape Canaveral that we wanted to stay in, and we did not want to rent the house out.

Cary and I finished mailing everything we wanted and did a final cleaning. There were still several boxes that Jim and Tish were going to pick up. The day before we left, we went to visit Mom and Dad one last time at the cemetery. I don't know when I will ever return there, so it was a special goodbye to them. We then went to one of my parents' favorite restaurants for an early dinner. The next day, Cary and I would board Amtrak for a leisurely cross-country train adventure to Florida.

Chapter 17:
Finding My Way Home to Florida

Sunday December 18, 2011

Cary and I traveled home to Florida by train. After riding from Florida to California by bicycle, I didn't want to just fly home. I wanted another adventure! The Amtrak train from Oxnard, California to Orlando, Florida seemed like another fun adventure. Before we left, I took one more walk around and through my family home of 59 years. I figured it would probably sell, so I said my goodbyes to all those years as a cab took us to the downtown Oxnard Amtrak station. There, we boarded a commuter train to Los Angeles and then transferred to the Southwest Chief with a destination of Chicago, Illinois.

I surprised Cary with a Superliner Roomette in one of the sleeper cars. I couldn't imagine sitting in a regular train seat for four nights, so I splurged on the small room. It was actually very comfortable with a large picture window, two reclining seats which converted to a lower bed with an upper berth, a fold down table, reading lights, climate control, and even turn-down service and bed make-up in the mornings. There were bathrooms (a little larger than a plane's) and a shower room nearby. We were on the bottom of the two-level sleeper car with the dining car attached behind us and the dome lounge car right after that. With the attendant's help, we quickly settled in and found our way to the dining car for dinner. Since space is so limited, dining room guests are seated together with two on each side of the table. In this way, you make new friends quickly. We were fine with this arrangement for most of the sittings, but there were a few times we would have liked to change company. It was all fun though.

After dinner, we sat in our roomette and opened the first of six bottles of wine we had brought. Alcohol is allowed in the sleeper cars but not in the passenger cars. Soon it was dark, so the attendant made up our beds and we fell asleep in the gently rolling train.

Monday December 19, 2011

I was up early as I didn't want to miss any of the scenery. I separated the lower berth back into two reclining seats and sat to watch the country go by. I have always enjoyed trains, but until now I had never taken the time to enjoy one like this. When Cary got up, we went back to the dining car for a delicious breakfast and were joined by the gentleman in the roomette across from ours. The menu was limited but the selections good. When we returned to our roomette, it was already made up by our attendant. We spent the morning talking with our neighbor, checking our email (with my MiFi, as this train didn't have WiFi), reading, and napping. Cary stared out at the moving landscape and drew. After lunch, we watched a Three Stooges DVD on my laptop as we enjoyed more wine. What a life! From California, we entered Arizona by way of Kingman and then to Gallup, New Mexico. There was word of a blizzard heading west along the plains, so when we arrived in Albuquerque, New Mexico we changed engines for one with a snow plow. As the snow continued to build, we lost more time. Monday evening we entered Colorado from the town of Trinidad. After dinner we enjoyed more conversation and wine with our neighbor before we were gently lulled to sleep.

Tuesday, December 20, 2011

In the middle of the night, I woke up because I felt the train stop. Through the dim light I noticed huge drifts of snow. After a few hours we were moving again, so I drifted back to sleep. When dawn appeared, we were stopped again. During breakfast we were told that the drifts were so high the train had to stop. The engine continued to have problems so we stopped and replaced it once again in Kansas. At that stop, we left the car for a few minutes to stand in the snow. By this time we were several hours behind our scheduled arrival time in Chicago of 3:00 P.M. Our connecting train to Washington D.C. was scheduled to leave Chicago at 7:00 P.M. We sat in the large window dome lounge and enjoyed the beautiful countryside covered in snow. As the blizzard grew worse, we continued to go slower. We sat up most of the night and napped before finally arriving in Chicago at 2:00 A.M. Wednesday.

Wednesday December 21, 2011

Everybody who was scheduled for a connecting train proceeded to the Amtrak Customer Service Office where we were told that buses would take us to Washington, DC. We really didn't want to take a bus that far, so I worked my way inside the office and told the staff that we were going all the way to Florida. Amtrak was very accommodating and gave us a voucher for a hotel, cab, and food. By 3:00 A.M., we were settled into a very nice hotel in downtown Chicago on the 26th floor. When we woke up at 8:00 A.M., the view overlooking downtown and Lake Michigan was amazing. We left the hotel and took a cab back to Union Station where we were fortunately able to obtain reservations on the 7:00 P.M. train to Washington D.C. That left us several hours to explore downtown Chicago.

After breakfast, we walked around to see the sights. Unfortunately, we were not dressed right for the drizzling rain and cold. We walked around until Cary saw a sign for an ancient Asian Artwork Store/ Museum. Since he is very interested in this period's art, we hailed a cab and were soon there. We spent a few hours walking around in awe of the intricate artwork. After that, we walked around until we came to an old corner bar and grill that looked like it had some history to it. We enjoyed a few beers and an excellent sandwich before continuing our wandering. Soon, we were back at Union Station and boarded the Capital Limited passenger car. We did have reservations for a roomette on yesterday's train, but there were none available on today's. I could not get comfortable in the reclining seat and ended up reading and napping in the lounge car while Cary was fine with his seat.

Thursday December 22, 2011

We were up with the sun enjoying the Maryland countryside and bought breakfast in the lounge car's snack shop. In fact, I stayed in the lounge car until we pulled into Union Station, Washington D.C. at 11:00 A.M. I was really enjoying this pace of traveling and seeing the country. The train to Orlando didn't leave until 7:00 P.M., so we had another several hours to explore. We walked out of Union Station, and I immediately saw the Capital Building off in the distance, and soon we were on the National Mall and had the time to explore all the monuments. First up was an excellent lunch at a local pub before setting off for the World War II Memorial. The last time Andee and I were here was in 1981 when there were fewer memorials. Cary and I toured the WWII, Vietnam, and Korean War Memorials. Then we walked to the Lincoln Memorial and leisurely made our way back to Union Station. Cary sat in the waiting lounge while I sat in a Union Station bar and enjoyed a few beers. At 6:00 P.M., we boarded the Silver Meteor and quickly settled into another comfortable roomette for the 17-hour ride to Orlando.

Friday December 23, 2011

At dawn, we were in South Carolina and enjoyed a leisurely breakfast in the dining car. I went back to the lounge car and viewed the countryside as we traveled through Georgia and into Florida. I called Andee and told her we would be at the Orlando Station around 1:00 P.M. That gave us time for one last meal in the dining car. I could really get used to this type of travel. However, I would not want to travel across the country in a passenger car. The cost for a roomette is an extra thousand or so but well worth it. It is a wonderful and comfortable way to see the country. We soon arrived on time and were greeted by Andee and Jocelyn. After four months of traveling, my family was together again for a Merry Christmas indeed!

Epilogue

I spent the month of January enjoying my outdoor lifestyle back on the beach. Jocelyn made a temporary move to Colorado Springs to help take care of Andee's aunt. I still missed the daily biking routine with her and eventually shipped the Surly so that she could continue her riding in Colorado. She seemed happy out there, as she was trying to figure out the next stage in her life. At the beginning of February, I was notified that all my medical, psychological, and dental testing was complete and satisfactory, so I began planning for my next adventure in Antarctica. With some regret and trepidation, I left home again on February 10 and flew to Christchurch, New Zealand. Three days later I was on the ice in McMurdo Station, Antarctica.

I am working for a NASA contractor at a remote satellite tracking station. My job is to operate and maintain a 10-meter dish antenna along with all the associated equipment required to track polar orbiting satellites and the distribution of the downlinked data. It is an exciting job on a very harsh but beautiful continent. We are currently in a dark Antarctic winter with the next sunrise anticipated August 20th. This duty is for eight months, so I should return home by mid-October, 2012.

We dipped our front tires in the Pacific Ocean

Part 2:

New Zealand

A Father and Daughter Adventure Continues: A Six Week Bicycle Journey Around the South Island of New Zealand

After spending eight months on the ice at McMurdo Station, Antarctica, I returned to Christchurch, New Zealand on Friday October 5, 2012 after a nice 5 hour flight from the sea-ice Pegasus runway in Antarctica.

I wrote Part 1 of this book while spending the Austral Winter on the ice. I am happy and sad to be leaving as no one ever really knows if they will return to the Antarctic. It has been a wonderful adventure and privilege to have spent eight months of my life experiencing an Antarctic winter. What a world!

The Antarctic is beautiful, grueling, and unforgettable — it can take your breath away. This is what I will miss:

The beautiful super-clear air and sky.

The Transantarctic Mountains and the Royal Society Mountain Range.

Pods of whales cruising through McMurdo Sound at the end of summer.

The solid ice shelf across McMurdo Sound that forms in the winter.

The sun which circles around Antarctica and never sets in a 24 hour period.

The Southern Cross which circles the dark sky and never goes away.

Total darkness 24 hours a day.

Thousands of stars 24 hours a day.

Dazzling colorful auroras fading in and out of the Antarctic sky.

The moon circling Antarctica.

Driving a Pisten Bully tracked vehicle across the glacial ice.

Building igloos.

The unique sunrise and sunset.

Watching seals crawl out of the water and lay on the ice all day. It's amazing that they can exit freezing water and lie out in way colder air and act as if they are comfortable as they bask on the ice.

Watching penguins spend several minutes trying to jump out of the water, miss, and then finally landing onto the ice. Once on the ice, they look around for a few seconds and then jump back in the water. What are they thinking?

Meeting many new friends and sharing dinner and a bottle of wine.

Running from building to building when it is super cold outside.

The cold Antarctic katabatic wind that slams down the surrounding hills and shakes the buildings.

Going for a long Sunday hike up Observation Hill, across the Ross Glacier, or one of the various other trails, and then returning to my room for a long, hot shower, after which I drink a cold beer and fall asleep for a nice nap.

Watching the nacreous clouds dance high in the sky.

Driving up the hill in a Pisten Bully to work after a storm.

Sitting in the dorm lounge with several friends, sharing beer and popcorn, and watching some dumb movie for the tenth time. What critics we were!

Dodging Skua birds as they try to steal everything you are carrying.

The polar plunge: jumping into 28 degrees F seawater with the surrounding temperature at minus 55 degrees F.

An aurora alert page at 0200 from the firehouse. Getting all bundled up and going outside for the beautiful light show. Knowing that it is too cold to take pictures but that the memory will last forever in my mind. Crawling back in bed with a huge smile.

Getting help from a friend when feeling depressed and helpless and then retuning the favor knowing that we all are in the same boat.

Walking to Captain Robert Falcon Scott's Discovery Hut Point and staring at the great expanse along the coastline.

Being the first one at dinner and sitting at my usual table. Then all of a sudden I am joined by five others and it turns into a small party.

Getting blown down by the wind, and then getting up and laughing.

Friday after dinner shopping at Walmart (aka 'The Store').

Shoveling snow.

Watching movies in the Coffee House Theater. Bringing in a beer or sharing a bottle of wine while watching with friends.

Hosting "Surfing Night in Antarctica" on Thursday evenings in the dead of winter. What a hoot! It is just what we needed: travel, sun, surf, sand, and bikinis.

Sunday evenings at the Coffee House Theater for McMurdo Science Theater 3000 aka "Movies so bad they are good". Everybody in the audience is a critic who blurted out the funniest comments.

Enjoying a cup of hot chocolate at the Coffee House Bar on Sunday nights with friends.

Visiting Kiwi friends on "American Nights at Scott Base" (New Zealand's Antarctic Station — a few miles from McMurdo). Enjoying a few Guinness and frivolity in the pub.

Getting so excited about "freshies" when the first plane arrived after a long winter. I will never walk into a grocery store produce/fruit section again without thinking about McMurdo.

Hearing people laugh in the galley even though we are all a little depressed or down at times because we miss our families.

Going to a winter party. The live music was way too loud, but it was super fun. The cold and windy walk back to the dorm had a sobering effect.

Having breakfast, lunch, and dinner prepared along with no clean up.

Just simply looking at the landscape and sky in awe.

The freedom: no badges, wallets, cell phones, keys or locks, cars, and just taking care of myself.

The complete silence of the Antarctic when the wind stops.

An Antarctic adventure has ended, and another Father and Daughter Adventure is set to start. The pilot announced that the cockpit was open for visitors for the amazing flight over the Antarctic continent. There were only 15 of us redeploying, so we all had ample time for the experience. Soon, New Zealand came into view along with something else we all had been missing — green! We saw trees for the first time in eight months! My first smell when I stepped off the plane was a humid smell of pending rain. How sweet that was, and it did start raining as we disembarked. After customs and luggage collection, we stopped off at the United States Antarctic Program Clothing Distribution Center to drop off our three bags of Extreme Cold Weather (ECW) Gear. I was very happy to get rid of all those clothes that I have been wearing daily for the past eight months, especially the heavy parka, since I am a shorts, T-shirt, and sandals guy. Once that was complete, we were taken to our motels in Christchurch. During the shuttle ride, all was quiet as we took in the sights of trees, flowers, dogs walking, and children playing in the parks of Christchurch, and of course, city traffic. All the sights and smells were so welcome.

McMurdo Station at winter's end 2012

The next morning, I hopped on a Christchurch Metro Bus for a run to a local mall and Vodaphone store. There I purchased a prepaid phone and USB Internet stick for mobile broadband (MiFi). Neither Jocelyn's nor my phone would work here, so this was a cheap alternative for making calls home or for advance reservations at campsites and backpackers (hostels). The Kiwis travel a lot on weekends, so these accommodations are sometimes booked well in advance. The MiFi will come in handy when WiFi is not available. We also had a MiFi on our 2011 U.S. cross-country trip. It makes my updates on crazyguyonabike.com and Jocelyn's "Believe the Ride" on Facebook easier and more convenient than waiting for WiFi areas.

That afternoon, I moved to Point Break Backpackers in New Brighton Beach on the Christchurch coast where I stayed until our ride began. It is a cool hostel (New Zealand backpackers are hostels.), very friendly and accommodating at only $50 for a twin room with shared bathroom, and as I had been living in a small dorm room with shared bathroom at McMurdo Station for the last eight months, this was fine. I like the easy and "bumming style". An ice friend of mine, Will, was also staying there before starting his "off the ice" adventures. Most people returning from the ice like to travel before returning home. It is an ideal situation since you are halfway around the world anyway, so why not explore?

I emailed a friend of mine from the ice and gave her my new phone number. Gracie and her husband Kevin left McMurdo a week earlier than I did and were camping around the South Island, so we were going to try and meet up. After getting settled into my room, I walked the short distance to the beach. The beach at New Brighton is very clean and beautiful. The coastal area reminded me of my hometown beach in Oxnard, California. I immediately felt at peace since I am a beach guy and back where I belong. A short time later I heard a noise coming from my pocket — it was my new phone ringing — and my first call! What a strange sound, as there is no cell phone service on the ice! Gracie was calling to tell me that several ice people were meeting at a place called Dux Live near downtown Christchurch that evening. I thought that would be fun and so did Will, so we hailed a taxi and met our ice friends for dinner and delicious locally brewed beer from Dux Live Brewery. We were soon bar hopping down the streets of Christchurch on a Saturday night. After an entertaining first night back in civilization, Will and I returned by taxi to our rooms.

The following day, we hopped on the Metro bus system to explore Christchurch and the surrounding communities. We ended up on the coast north of New Brighton Beach in the small community of Sumner Beach. It was refreshing to walk through the water and see families playing and surfing. After lunch, we found our way back to New Brighton Beach by way of downtown Christchurch. Damage from the massive earthquake of February 2011 was still very real. But in the eight months since I was here, there had been much more demolition, but more importantly, reconstruction. The resourcefulness of the Kiwis with rebuilding was very evident and encouraging. I spent the rest of the day exploring New Brighton Beach.

. Before I left the ice, I'd started the process toward a new job at the South Pole for the Austral Winter of 2013. This entailed physical qualifying (PQ) with much more detail than my McMurdo position. I started the process at McMurdo medical with a National Science Foundation (NSF) polar physical and dental examination. I scheduled my required blood work and abdominal ultrasound in Christchurch for the Monday and Tuesday before

Jocelyn's arrival on Wednesday. The ultrasound was new to me and is a requirement for those wintering at the South Pole to make sure everything looks normal in the gallbladder (no gallstones) and other abdominal organs. I am writing this from Amundsen-Scott South Pole Station (840 miles from McMurdo Station which is on the coast) in February 2013 after having arrived here mid-January, so obviously I passed the extensive medical, dental, and psychological testing. It will be another long winter for me, as the station is now closed and due to reopen for the Austral Summer in early November. It is such an honor and privilege to be living this South Pole winter adventure with 43 other people, and I am the 1,385th person to winter here since 1957. The South Pole station sits on two miles of ice at an altitude of 9,300 feet. The physiological altitude changes daily with the barometric pressure and ranges from 9,500 to 11, 500 feet. The record low temperature is -117 degrees F and along with the windchill can easily go below -140 degrees F.

After my Monday appointment, I went to Natural High Bicycle Adventure shop near the Christchurch Airport. I had been in contact with them several months before for our bike hire and had reservations for two bikes along with camping gear. There, I met Sandra who showed me the bikes. I chose a Specialized bike instead of the selected Cannondale, because with my riding style I prefer a straight bar over the drop bars. I test rode it around the parking lot and was pleased with the fit. Jocelyn was bringing out our Brookes leather saddles and seat posts so I didn't bother with any seat fitting. I was also pleased with the professional advice from Sandra and talked at length with her on our planned route. She had cycled over much of the South Island so she had many recommendations. Her local knowledge was a real bonus. After purchasing several maps, I returned to Brighton Beach.

The next day I had another medical appointment, where I ran into another ice friend also going through the PQ process for the next winter. She also passed, and I saw her in McMurdo as I was passing through in January.

Jocelyn arrived in Christchurch, New Zealand right on time after a 13 hour flight from San Francisco followed by another quick flight from

Auckland. I purchased her a surprise upgrade to Premium Economy. She had really enjoyed that and I didn't realize there was quite a difference on Air New Zealand. For the round trip it was only an additional $600. We will both fly Premium Economy going home. It is worth it for the much larger reclining seat and the excellent food and drink service.

It was a quick taxi ride to Natural High Bike Shop. Sandra sized Jocelyn on a Cannondale touring bike. Jocelyn brought out all of our panniers and most of our biking tools and equipment. We unloaded our panniers, aerobars, saddles, and other gear that Natural High installed, along with mud-flaps, mirrors, and bike computers. A camping outfit delivered our camping gear. After that, we went to an outdoors store where I purchased wind/rain pants along with new and studier sandals for water use. Across the street was Speight's Ale House where we split a fish and chips lunch, after which we found the Metro Bus nearby and returned to Brighton Beach. We were both raring to go and moved up our departure date to Friday.

Jocelyn and I spent Thursday touring around Christchurch by foot and the Metro Bus. Christchurch has an excellent botanical garden which we enjoyed immensely. Downtown we walked around the new Re:Start Container Mall. This area was devastated during the 2011 earthquake, and after demolition many stores had shipping containers built and stacked to sell their wares from. This area now has a huge mall built of these containers. We purchased some last-minute traveling items and then boarded a bus to the outskirts of Christchurch to an excellent lunch spot, which had been recommended by Sandra, called Cassels and Sons Brewery. While there, we sampled their excellent home brews along with a pizza. Soon, it was back to New Brighton Beach where we packed up a duffel bag that I would store at the Antarctic Center and also sorted through what we would tour with. Will met us for dinner at an excellent restaurant on the beach. Then, it was to bed early dreaming once again of another Father and Daughter Adventure.

"Turn your face to the sun and the shadows fall behind you."

– old Maori proverb

Day 1: October 12th – Christchurch to Amberley

We arrived at Natural High at 10:00 A.M. after a quick stop at the Antarctic center to drop off a duffel bag, and then we proceeded to dump out all our stuff on four tables to sort what to pack in our panniers. What a mess! It reminded me of the prepacking for our cross-country trip in 2011. Jeremy continued to set up our bikes. He had most of our equipment installed but everything needed adjustments.

It took a lot longer than we thought to pack. After that, our hire paperwork was completed and we were finally on the road at 2:00 P.M. The four hours just flew by and was actually fun to get us in the biking mood. You could not have erased the smiles on our faces as we rode down the street. It was such a pleasure to be on the road again — especially together! It didn't take long to get used to riding on the other side of the road, but you really have to look both ways all the time. The "give ways" can be very confusing, and there aren't that many stop signs. We headed north on the recommended roads that paralleled Hwy 1. Sandra and the owner of Natural High, Andy, both thought that we should be able to make Amberley for the evening. Just as in our cross-country trip, we did not have a day-to-day schedule — wherever we ended up for the day was an unknown.

We stopped for lunch at Monty's Fish and Chips in the small town Kaiapoi. The cafe advertised "Fresh Whitebait Patties". We didn't know what it was, but the server said they were a delicacy only available certain times of the year and that we should try it. I did, and it was the first of many seafood items in which we would partake while in the country. Whitebait is caught in nets during high tide when the seawater is flowing into rivers and inlets. These tiny, boneless fish are clumped together and pan fried as a patty and served over a slice of bread. It really is delicious if you can look past all the beady black eyes staring at you. While eating, the radio announcer said that tomorrow's weather was going to be miserable and to put on a fire and a stew. Before we'd left Natural High, Andy said there was a system dropping down to the South Island bringing rain, strong winds, and cold. At that point, we decided that we didn't want to camp the first night, so after passing a few 'no vacancies' at local pubs, we opted for a motel room inside Amberley Campground. It was only four hours and 31 miles up the road but with increasing headwinds. We moved the bikes inside the spacious room, and since we'd just packed everything, only a few items were removed.

We explored our first town and decided on a local pub where we enjoyed the busy atmosphere along with a simple snack of nachos. After the beef nachos, we went on our planned vegetarian trip, except for one time when I just had to try "Bangers and Mash". The bartender said, "Those nachos will make you pedal your bike," and, "It's only uphill from here, mate!" when I told him we were headed around the South Island. It was a good day, and it felt great to be back on a bike. One year ago we were on our cross-country U.S. trip. It's great to be back on the saddle!

The start of our New Zealand adventure

Day 2: October 13th –
a Non-riding Weather Day in Amberley

Yesterday we had heard about a storm system moving down to the South Island, so we knew that riding today was going to be questionable. I was up early checking the weather forecast on the Internet and also on the TV news. When the weather guy said that the weather was going to be "Hideous with gale force winds" today, I figured that was it. It didn't really look that bad outside, but overnight there were occasional very strong gusts buffeting our room. And sure enough, by mid-morning it was raining hard sidewise from the northwest. I am sure glad we started our ride a day early and that we found this room. We visited another local pub where we enjoyed a few pints and played a game of darts. It was nice standing next to the large, open fireplace as it was very cold outside. October is still early spring in New Zealand. We then walked across the street and had an early dinner at a local cafe before stopping off at the local grocery store and back to the motel.

This trip isn't about a destination but the journey. We are not on any kind of schedule, so we are fine with the weather. And besides, the rain is what makes New Zealand so beautiful. Along with that, the people have been super nice and friendly. Tomorrow we will head 50 miles up the hill northwest to Hamner Springs that is famous for its hot springs. Originally we were not going to travel there, but after talking with a few locals we decided to.

Day 3: October 14th – Amberley to Culverden

The weather looked good this morning, so we were on the road by 7:00 A.M. It was cold but that was expected, so we dressed appropriately. About a mile out of town, I heard a noise from the front of my bike so we pulled over. The front rack bracket that attaches to the main post had bent and dropped the rack onto the tire. A nice Kiwi gentleman driving by pulled over and asked if we needed help. He said he had tools and would stand by until we were back on the road. With the Kiwi's help we were able to bend it back up, and I fortunately had several zip ties on hand to strap the rack up to reduce the load. He was also going to Hanmer and asked if we would like a lift. I politely declined even though it was very cold and windy. We were back on the road, but about 5 miles later the rack again collapsed. At this point, I removed the rack along with the weak bracket and then reattached the rack legs and the top with zip ties. That did the trick and we were back on the road. We did have several problems with brakes rubbing on the wheels, but after several stops and adjustments we continued.

To say that the countryside was beautiful would be an understatement. It was absolutely gorgeous riding up the hills and seeing snow on the surrounding mountains. This land reminds me so much of Hawaii as it is so green everywhere. The sheep, horses, and cows added to the atmosphere.

At noon, we were in the tiny town of Waikari and stopped at the local pub for a sandwich and fresh milk. After that, we continued through the amazing scenery and stopped for a wine tasting at Hurunui Vineyards. At this point, we had ridden by many vineyards so we just had to stop. The sun was finally shining and the clouds were gone, so we stopped and entered the tasting room where we each had four small samples. We then relaxed with a glass of wine along with a bread and dip appetizer. Life is good. We talked with the owner who said he wouldn't recommend riding to Hanmer today because it is up the hill on a very winding road with weekend traffic but that we should stay in the town of Culverden. Since we were running late because of mechanical problems, this looked like a good option. The GPS found the Culverden Motel and I gave them a call. They are in a campground, but the proprietor said that it has been freezing the last two nights and unless we were used to the cold their motel room was warmer. I have lived in the Antarctic for the last eight months but did not have the appropriate clothing to camp in this weather. After purchasing a bottle of delicious Pinot Noir from the winery, we continued on to Culverden. Once there, we signed in for one of the 6 rooms in this nice area, did our laundry in the sink, and laid it outside on chairs. We then chilled for the rest of the afternoon after having ridden only 30 miles which seemed much longer with rack bracket and brake problems. During this ride, we'd encountered New Zealand's infamous Magpie birds. The birds are very territorial and will strike at riding bicyclists if they come too close. I have read that they draw blood while beaking the person. Jocelyn had two strikes while I had none. Maybe it was our helmet colors.

New Zealand's beautiful countryside

Quiet roads

Day 4: October 15th – Culverden to Hanmer Springs

We were up early and I was ready to ride, but I had forgotten about a Skype appointment with my wife Andee. I have never used Skype before and I really wasn't interested, but Jocelyn did talk with her mom for quite a while. I was busy wanting to get on the road. So by the time we did pull out, the sunny morning gave way to clouds and wind. I figured we didn't have too far to go as it was only 20 miles to Hanmer Springs. It was a nice Monday morning but the weather was threatening, so we didn't stop much except for more sheep and cow pictures.

The climbing was easy to 1,200 feet as we passed many sheep farms and vineyards. The last few miles were very narrow and twisty, as we rode across a huge gorge full of swiftly moving water. The backdrop was the snow-covered Southern Alps. I'm glad we didn't attempt this on the vehicle-crowded weekend. We rolled into Hanmer Springs around noon and found Hanmer Backpackers. It was a really laid back and cool place to stay. Since there are many activities in town, we decided to stay two nights. We also decided to lose the camping gear as it was really slowing us down, and with the coldness, camping didn't seem too inviting. We mailed the rented gear back to Natural High and mailed whatever camping gear Jocelyn had brought back home to Florida. Traveling should be a lot easier now, and we don't want to miss anything. After talking with the German proprietor of Hanmer Backpackers, we decided that we would utilize the many backpackers around the island. I really like the atmosphere and the many interesting people from around the world that visit them. At $50 for a twin room, the price was right.

The Southern Alps

Day 5: October 16th A Non-riding Tourist Day

The previous night, we had a delicious meal and more excellent beer at Monteith's Brewery Pub. We sampled several excellent flavors along with many appetizers. Monteith's Brewery is in the West Coast town of Greymouth, so we put that on our list of must stops. In the morning, we visited the hot springs commercial pools area. I was disappointed that the actual 'Hanmer Springs' was so commercialized. The facility consisted of many pools of varying temperatures and mineral makeup. It was nice to finally get warm, but the atmosphere just turned me off. The spring's water source of long ago was still there, but I would rather it be more natural. We spent a few hours moving from one pool to another. After that, we had lunch at a popular and good pub before relaxing at the backpacker for the rest of the day. We bought groceries and cooked our dinner while conversing with many guests from around the world.

Day 6: October 17ᵗʰ – Hanmer Springs to Kaikoura

We left Hanmer after a leisurely-cooked breakfast. It was Jocelyn's 22ⁿᵈ birthday so she cooked for her dad! We rolled out of town after nine in a hard blow. There is nothing like a few steep hills and hard wind to wake you up. It took us two hours to backtrack to Hwy 70 where we turned north. It was there where I had my first flat. As you know after reading part 1 of this book, flats were a sore subject with Jocelyn as she had seven of them while I had only one, and that was just 200 miles from San Diego. I had almost made it across the entire country without one. So this first one for me was a bit alarming and I thought Jocelyn was going to tease me to no end, but she was silent although I did see a few smirks.

We had a pleasantly quiet ride to Rotherham where we stopped at the town's only pub for lunch with the locals. When we told them that we were headed to Kaikoura, they all looked at each other and laughed. "Have fun on that," they said. Shortly after that, we rode into hill country and thought about those people laughing. I guess they knew. We had a real go at it and it was unrelenting. I looked at my map and GPS, and we decided to stop at a lodge in Mt. Lyford for an accommodation. Well, the hills became little mountains, and with the little traffic on the road we wondered if the lodge would even be open on a weekday. We didn't have a phone number, so we pressed on until we saw the 3ʳᵈ car for the afternoon coming up a hill. It was a truck and Jocelyn flagged the driver down. A very nice gentleman was heading to Kaikoura and offered to take us there. It was getting late and Kaikoura was about 20 miles away.

We passed the lodge and the sign said open, but there were no cars around, so I'm glad we got a lift as that was the only accommodation until Kaikoura.

We talked at length about the sheep and farming business. The little mountains turned into big ones. I think we would still be there if not for Frasier. He dropped us off on the quay of Kaikoura at 5:00 P.M., and we found a bike shop that was still open to readjust the brakes that I had misadjusted. Bike brakes seem so simple, yet I have never really figured them out. After that, we found a nice motel across the street from the beach. After laundry and cleaning up, we celebrated Jocelyn's birthday with a few pints and dinner. The walk along the ocean was simply amazing with a backdrop of snow-covered mountains and a beach full of driftwood. The sea was calm and beautiful after the sunset. Then it was straight to bed. Tomorrow we want to try and reach Peddlers' Rest Backpackers in Ward, which is north along the coast for 50 miles. "Peddler's Paradise" — a cycle touring guide to New Zealand's South Island by Nigel Rushton highly recommends the accommodation.

Jocelyn's 22nd birthday

Day 7: October 18th – Kaikoura to Ward

This morning we were greeted by the sun and a very hard northwest wind. The morning news said the gusts were 70 mph, so we thought about staying put but decided to give it a go. We were being buffeted all over the road and ended up walking so we wouldn't get hit. Frasier had told us the winds can be ferocious. That was an understatement. A wide-load truck with six huge rain barrels passed us, and we saw it turn over about a quarter of a mile up the road. A huge gust got under it and just put it on its side. The road was closed for quite a while as work crews brought in a large crane to right the truck. We were finally able to pass and continued walking. A policeman stopped to talk with us and felt bad that we were having such a struggle. At this point two Finnish girls were riding into Kaikoura, so we and the policeman crossed the road and talked with them about the conditions further north. They said it was better on the coast and not as windy since the mountains were blocking the wind. After I told them we were headed there, they also said they stayed at Peddlers' Rest Backpackers two nights ago and had a great time. A few miles up the road, the coast turned more north and the wind stopped as it was blocked by the west mountain range.

Sandra from Natural High had mentioned that the coast north of Kaikoura was "simply stunning". I couldn't have said it better! We really enjoyed the beautiful mountains to the sea vistas. There was very little traffic so we were able to really enjoy the ride. We stopped at a trailer on the beach for a fresh lobster lunch. After that, we rode into fur seal country where we hiked 1,000 feet to a waterfall with a swimming area full of Ohau Stream Seal Pups. What a cool spot.

Hill country soon started again along with the headwinds, although not as bad as Kaikoura. We were both becoming weak and finally spotted the Peddlers' Rest bicycle sign. We turned off the coast road and were led a mile down a gravel road to a beautiful house with a cyclist bunkhouse nearby. The host warmly greeted us and showed us our bunkroom for the night. This bunkhouse was an old sheep shearing barn, so it had a very interesting setup. After we showered and did laundry, we walked back to the house where the owners maintain a store for travelers, including beer. Jocelyn cooked up a delicious canned spaghetti dinner that we enjoyed while sitting next to a roaring fireplace. We then walked around outside where we were greeted by several friendly dogs.

Most of the New Zealand biking blogs I have read talk about daily mileage of around 60 km (about 36 miles). At first I thought that was low, but I now realize that we don't want to go much over that because of the terrain and the weather. Plus there is a lot to see. We will continue north tomorrow.

Riding north along the Kaikoura coast

Lunch on the beach

A fur seal pup has Jocelyn's attention

Day 8: October 19th – Ward to Blenheim

We slept like babies in the bunkhouse, as it was just the two of us with occasional unknown animal noises. A few times we added wood to the fireplace. After a leisurely breakfast, Jocelyn added a long entry into the hosts' logbook. Last night we read through several of the books that date back to 1995.

We were soon on the road at 9:00 A.M. and had our early-morning hill workouts as we climbed to the small town of Ward. But this time the wind was at our backs!

We continued many more hill climbs through the sparsely-trafficked roads and miles of vineyards and soon entered the town of Seddon where we had lunch. One of the locals asked us where we were going. When we said Blenheim, he said, "No worries; hills are done." We climbed into one last large hill and the mountain pass that descends into Blenheim. The descent was exhilarating, and I worked the brakes to keep the speed below 35mph on a lane without a shoulder. It was a white-knuckle experience! As we rode into town, the wind picked up and thunderstorms started. We found the Koanui Backpackers and checked in to a very nice hostel room.

We had planned on riding to Picton and touring Queen Charlotte Sound, but we decided that we wanted to spend more time in the Nelson and Abel Tasman National Park areas. Also, Picton is the South Island ferry destination from the North Island and so is a very busy city. We found the bus station and made reservation for the bus to Nelson. It is Labor Day holiday weekend and the roads are crowded and the weather not very good. We had also read that the mountain road to Nelson is very narrow with lots of traffic. It was not recommended for cyclists.

We have now completed a week of our adventure. The most prominent features are the hills, wind, sheep, and vineyards. But what we are most impressed with are the friendly and very helpful people.

Day 9&10: October 20&21 – Blenheim to Nelson by Bus and a Tourist Day

Our Nelson bus reservations were for 12:45 P.M., so we spent the morning taking my bike to a local shop for a front rack bracket replacement and then walking around and exploring Blenheim. It was a fun and leisurely morning. The bus arrived on time and was very crowded, but the driver didn't mind working the bikes and all the panniers into the luggage compartment. She was a real trooper, and between the two of us and removing the front wheels we got it all in.

The 72 mile ride through the mountains took about 2 ½ hours. The bike ride would have taken us two days, and except for one town of Havelock close to Blenheim there are no accommodations unless you are camping. Besides, the road is very narrow and winding, with little to no shoulder. We were glad to pass on that.

We arrived at the bus station in downtown Nelson. As I was reinstalling my front wheel, I heard a voice, "Can I help you with that?" I looked up, and it was my friend Dan from the ice — unbelievable! He and his wife Karen had been driving around New Zealand for a month, and they just happened to be where the bus stopped. We chatted for a while, and then Jocelyn and I loaded up the bikes and found our motel for the next two nights. It was close to downtown and overlooked the Maitai River. That evening, we walked through the downtown area and enjoyed the local home brews in various establishments along with a delicious dinner.

Sunday morning we had a nice, leisurely 30 mile ride around Nelson without the panniers. I cannot think of a better way to see a town. We ended up at Tahunanui Beach with a nice lunch along the Nelson Marina quay at the Boat Shed Cafe. Tomorrow we will travel about 45 miles to Marahau where we have reservations for a cabin hire at Abel Tasman National Park.

Street bicycle parking in Nelson

Day 11: October 22nd – Nelson to Marahau at Abel Tasman National Park

We were on the road at 9:30 and shortly pulled over to put on our rain gear for the steady drizzle. It let up after a few hours just in time for our hill work. The very small town of Tasman had a general store, so we stopped there for a quick sandwich and a nice talk with the proprietor. We asked him which route (the coastal or inland) was better for cyclists. He said it didn't matter because they are both full of hills — an honest answer indeed. We were soon in the larger town of Motueka which is the gateway to Abel Tasman National Park.

We continued up a mountain road that seemed to go on forever. There was a couple hiking the narrow two-lane road, and they said we were on the right track. We both ended up walking as it was very steep. It was about 9 miles through the Kaiteriteri Forest. Several mountain bikers passed us, and we got a lot of, "Good on you mate; that's a good climb." We finally leveled off at 750 feet and then had an exhilarating ride down the other side into the coastal park. At the end of the road in Marahau we found "The Barn", our backpacker for the next three nights. We checked in and were shown our tiny cabin. We both sat there and stared at each other and said this was cool. The cabin was actually a shed with a twin bed on each side. The front was a sliding glass door. There was a light but no outlets. It was a step above camping, and we enjoyed it. The bathrooms along with an outdoor kitchen were about 100 feet away. There was also a nearby building with interior rooms, another kitchen, and a fireplace.

Fortunately, the office sold beer and a little bit of food. Marahau is directly south of Abel Tasman National Park which is New Zealand's most adventurous national park. In fact, the hiking trail starts right next to The Barn. There was also an excellent restaurant called the Park Cafe nearby where we enjoyed fresh fish dinners.

A steep climb to Marahau

Shed camping at The Barn in Marahau

Day 12&13 October 23rd & 24th
Tourist Days at Abel Tasman

We spent three nights at The Barn, which gave us two full days to explore the park. The first morning I was up with the sun with a beautiful ocean sunrise. I then cooked some noodle soup with eggs at the outdoor kitchen. Last night we had walked to town and stopped by the local "Aqua Taxi" business to inquire about their services. We returned there and purchased tickets for the water taxi's first ride up the coast alongside Abel Tasman Park. They, along with a few other companies, provide a drop-off and pick-up service at any of the park's beaches. We rode the water taxi to the northernmost part of the park and then looped back to one of the beaches where we went ashore for a three hour hike south along the Abel Tasman Coast Track to a pick-up spot by a bay. The coast ride was beautiful with the ocean teaming with sea life, including many types of fish, rays, seals, and even small penguins. The hike reminded us of the Kalalau Trail at the end of the road on the north shore of Kauai, Hawaii. It was a sometimes challenging hike through a tropical rainforest setting with beautiful views of the coast. There was quite a bit of climbing, but with our cycling shape we met the challenge easily.

We passed several campers loaded down with gear who were really struggling. There were several narrow one-way swing bridges over streams that we crossed. Usually, to the west of these were beautiful waterfalls, sometimes with kayakers paddling upstream from the calm ocean. Kayaking is very popular here with the water taxis carrying people with their kayaks, dropping them off a few miles north, with them paddling back. Abel Tasman Park is all about adventure. There are also many challenging mountain biking trails. Camping is very rural in this beautiful setting, and everything taken in must be removed. Drinking water is scarce, but there are occasional sparse bathroom facilities. The rainforest is covered with ferns of all kinds, which is appropriate since New Zealand's national symbol is the silver fern. Around every corner of the hike there appeared seemingly hidden coves where one could be dropped off for a lazy afternoon and picnic. We had brought our lunch and enjoyed it while sitting on large rocks surrounded by a beautiful small cove.

After almost three hours, we arrived at the agreed upon pick-up bay. While waiting, we explored the beach and the numerous pieces of driftwood and shells. At that point the weather was threatening thunderstorms, but soon our water taxi arrived. It was a wet, rainy ride back to Marahau while plowing into the increasing seas. It is interesting how these taxis get in and out of the water. The tides in this area are around 15 feet, so there are tractors that travel on the tidal basin towing the boat out to the water and then out again. The passengers remain onboard the trip back to the business' parking lot and then disembark. It is a very interesting launching system. Once we arrived, we stopped off at the Park Cafe for happy hour, and then back to The Barn to clean up, and then back for dinner. We spent that evening at The Barn's inside kitchen and lounge area sitting by the fire, working on our web site updates, chatting with other guests, and enjoying a bottle of wine. What a nice day.

The next day we decided to take a break and just chill on the beach. We walked to the beginning of the Abel Tasman Coast Track and headed north. The trail goes on for 30 miles and takes 3-5 days to hike. After a mile or so, we found a nice, secluded beach and settled down for a few hours. We explored the many large rocks, beautiful expansive beach, read, napped, and enjoyed another picnic lunch. Since the tide was out, we walked back to Marahau across the flats and then through town and back to The Barn. Once again, we enjoyed a delicious fish dinner at the Park Café where we enjoyed four meals. After another evening in front of the fireplace, we retired early as we were anxious to get back on the road.

Hiking in Abel Tasman National Park

Day 14: October 25ᵗʰ Abel Tasman to Motueka

After three nights in Marahau it was time to move on. We took our time with breakfast and packing the bikes, so it was a late start for the return to Motueka. We had passed through Motueka four days before and mistakenly taken the inland hilly route to Marahau. Once at Marahau, we were told that the coastal route by way of Kaiteriteri Beach is still hilly but not as steep and is a prettier ride. We slowly worked our way back through the numerous beautiful coastal views. We enjoyed a stop at the golden sand beach in Kaiteriteri. The sand gets its gold color from crushed granite rock. We eventually merged onto the road we had traveled north on and arrived mid-afternoon in Motueka. We decided to stay at the Hat Trick Backpackers for the night as it was too late to make the run along the Motueka River Highway to the next accommodation — a campground in Tapawera. Next door to the backpackers was the Sprig and Fern Tavern which turned out to be another good dinner spot along with a few pints of their local brew. It seems that every tavern or pub in New Zealand has a few flavors of home brew. That night we played pool at an Irish bar with two guests, a Kiwi and a Frenchman, who we had met at the backpackers. Tomorrow we will begin our trek to the highly-anticipated West Coast.

Day 15: October 26th – Motueka to Tapawera

We had an early start after stopping at the local Motueka Café for breakfast. On the way to this café, I once again found myself on the wrong side of the road and was chided by a city worker. Usually Jocelyn catches me riding on the wrong side first. The ride south through the lush Motueka Valley was very pretty with farm and cattle land. The hours rolled by as we rode alongside the Motueka River. We passed by many hops farms, as this latitude of New Zealand is known as the hops capital of the country, and with such a varied beer selection, this hops industry is very important. In the early afternoon, we had reached our goal of the Settle Campground in Tapawera. Even though there was plenty of more riding time available, we decided to stay put because of the lack of accommodations/services on the way to St. Arnaud, and I had read that the ride itself to St Arnaud is all uphill. About an hour after we settled into our cabin, the south wind had picked up strong and the sky went overcast. So it was a good call all around. It was a short walk to the local grocery store, where I bought beer, our favorite New Zealand nacho chips, and a newspaper. Back at the camp, I sat on the patio and read the paper while Jocelyn napped. We then walked to the local pub for dinner. The campground had a lounge, a kitchen, and a dining area with a television. It was a real treat to watch a few local shows. We soon retired to our comfortable and quiet cabin and dreamed of climbing.

I have read about and experienced long bicycle journeys. One of the most special parts of a journey is the people you meet. This one is no exception. The proprietors of the backpackers, stores, tourist businesses, pubs, and restaurants all make this journey special. I can't think of a single negative thing about anyone we have met. They have all been so helpful and cheerful, and they go out of their way to give us their time when it comes to recommendations, especially about which routes to take. I have found that the most knowledgeable people to talk with are bus drivers, whether you are using their service or not. I have walked up to many of them with my map in hand asking questions about routes, accommodations, and services.

A beautiful ride along the Motueka River

Day 16: October 27th – Tapawera to St. Arnaud

We had our earliest start yet at 7:00 A.M. because the weather forecast called for rain. It was a quiet Saturday morning ride out of Tapawera on the Motueka Valley Hwy. We continued to State Hwy (SH) 6 for a few miles before we rejoined the Motueka Hwy to the resort area of St. Arnaud. We'd heard that this was a much quieter road than SH6, plus we would avoid the Hope Saddle which has a very steep elevation climb of

1,500 feet. The route we took was much higher but at a lower rise. Plus, we were only passed by about a dozen cars today — a very nice road. We traveled along many undulating hills, but we felt the steady climb in the cool mountain atmosphere. We stopped several times to take pictures of the numerous pine-forested valleys often surrounded by beautiful wildflowers. We had stocked up on food in Motueka, so we made a few snack stops to refuel for the continued climbing. It was unbelievable how few cars were traveling this road, especially on a beautiful Saturday. We took over the road and it was fun. While climbing, we had enough room to move back and forth to keep our momentum going through the steeper rises.

We only traveled 34 miles today but topped off at 2,400 feet. It was a steady climb for all of the 34 miles, and we didn't arrive in St Arnaud until 1:30 P.M. To only ride 34 miles in 6 hours seems pretty slow, but we were exhausted at that. We had reservations (one of the few times) at the Alpine Lodge in this ski resort area. It was nice to be in a comfortable motel room for a change. We were tired of being cold and sleeping on slim mattresses as we had for the past week. While Jocelyn talked with her mom, I walked to the nearby Lake Rotoiti along a rapidly moving stream. It was here that I was introduced to the infamous New Zealand sandfly. I had read that they don't like moving targets, so I kept up a good pace. It was a quick look at the lake because I was soon enveloped by these pests who swarm and attack. There were actually sandfly warning signs on the trail: "Don't stop...!" Across the street from the lodge was a small grocer, so I picked out a bottle of wine and cheese. After that, we enjoyed a nice dinner at the lodge along with a huge, roaring fire. If the weather holds, we are on to Murchison tomorrow.

Day 17: October 28th – St. Arnaud to Murchinson

I didn't wake up until after 7:00, so I guess I had been tired. After dinner last night, we stayed in the room as it was raining. Jocelyn woke up around 8:00, so we packed up and prepared for a rainy ride. After the continental breakfast at the lodge, we were on the road at 9:00. For the first two hours we rode through a steady rain. The traffic was pretty isolated on this Sunday morning until we reached the Kawatiri Junction where Hwy 63 meets SH6. From then on the traffic was flowing, and without a shoulder on the mountainous twisting road it was a bit difficult to take in the beautiful scenery. I had read that the West Coast's SH6 is a busy road but is the only way to travel the coast.

We quickly dropped several hundred feet in elevation, but there were plenty of ups and downs on the rolling mountainside. There were also a few exotic animal farms, so we stopped for pictures. About halfway through the day's ride, we came upon a hunter's camp/tavern called the Owen River Tavern, seemingly in the middle of nowhere, so we stopped in for a pint and a bowl of hot vegetable soup. They had a nice heater running, so we were able to warm up a bit. We each had a pint along with a bowl of vegetable soup and a few slices of bread. The total came to $39 NZ ($32 U.S.). Eating out in New Zealand is very expensive! But we got out of the rain and cold for a while.

We were soon at our goal of the small valley town of Murchison, but the backpackers we wanted to stay at, "The Lazy Cow", had a 'No Vacancy' sign. So we rode around a bit and found a cottage in this little town of paradise nestled between the mountains. Murchinson reminds me of Hawaii with all the greenery and colorful plants and flowers. It is like stepping back in time, as the downtown area is composed of old buildings with horses walking down the street. We have really found some cool spots to stay in. We ate in a local pub where I had my last red meat in the form of "Bangers and Mash". This dish consists of beef sausages, mashed potatoes, and peas all covered in gravy. I had been wanting to try this delicious dish, and it didn't disappoint. Jocelyn kept giving me the "Why are you eating that?" look. That was the last of the meat for the trip. We had wanted to walk around the town, but a rain shower appeared, so we ran back to the cottage. Since Westport is about 60 mountainous miles away, we retired early. Our map didn't show any accommodations along the way.

A wet ride alongside the Buller River

One of the many one-way bridges we crossed that day

Day 18: October 29ᵗʰ – Murchinson to Westport

We had another early start, as this was going to be a long and challenging day. The day started off like the previous several days with lots of climbing. But the sun was shining bright, so we had fun. We have our climbing legs now so we are used to it. But this day was different, as the ups and downs never stopped. A few miles out of town, we stopped at the longest swing bridge in New Zealand. Since we are tourists, we said, "Why not?" The usual charge just to walk across the Buller River Gorge is $5, but the guy working there said anyone who bicycles here is free. It was fun but a bit unnerving due to the swinging. We continued along SH6 with increasing truck traffic. Our new nemeses were the dairy trucks. I had read that they don't slow down or move over for cyclists. We confirmed that really quickly. There were so many one way bridges that we lost count. In-between the traffic it was a really beautiful ride. We stopped in a picnic/camping area and enjoyed a sandwich along with a glass of wine and fruit. Several people stopped by while we were there and questioned us about our trip. We never tired talking with people.

About halfway to Westport, in the small town of Inangahua, there was a backpacker that didn't look too inviting, so we decided to push on to Westport. We met a couple from Montana heading to Murchinson and had a nice chat with them. The scenery was ever-changing and beautiful as we had been paralleling the Buller River for two days now. As we neared Westport, the headwinds picked up considerably and we grew tired. After 9 hours and 60 miles, we finally made it to Westport and stopped at the first motel we saw. After a quick shower and laundry, we visited a local tavern for a few pints and pizza. Soon, the tavern was taken over by a local rugby team that had just won a championship the day before and was partying. A few of them struck up a conversation with us, so after another pint we left for a well-deserved rest. Tomorrow we will start our trek down the West Coast.

A nice picnic lunch

Day 19: October 30th – Westport to Punakaiki

We finally left Westport at 9:00 A.M. after a leisurely breakfast and topping off the tires at the local Firestone Auto Shop. Since yesterday had been such a long day, we really were not in a riding mood but didn't want to stay in Westport another night. Our goal was the Punakaiki Beach Backpackers for a two-night rest. We encountered multiple steep hills, some with up to three peaks. We would get over one peak only to see another one coming up. It was quite a challenge, but when we finally made it to the coast the view was simply stunning. We had heard that the West Coast was one of the most popular New Zealand rides, and we could see why. It was beautiful as we rode along this South Pacific paradise. Palm trees lined the roadside while the shoreside was scattered with little islands, some with tree growth. Surf was up and broke along the rocky shore. At times, there were small, sandy beach areas that looked inviting except for the rough surf.

As we continued to ride the hills, we completely forgot about how tired we were and just enjoyed this awesome ride. After lunch at a scenic picnic spot high up on a bluff, we descended the last hill and arrived at another slice of paradise — the Punakaiki Beach Backpacker — which is directly on the beach. The proprietor recommended the front twin cottage with beautiful views and the sound of the crashing waves. At that point I said, "Two nights please."

Shortly after we arrived, a Canadian cycling couple also arrived from Westport after having left an hour after us. We enjoyed dinner and conversation with them at the one and only tavern in town. It was fun swapping New Zealand "Tales from the road". We continued to enjoy their company back at the hostel kitchen and dining room area late into the night. What a fine ride today. Tomorrow has been declared a rest day after five straight days on the road. We fell asleep to sound of the waves crashing on the shore.

October 31st was a rest day. After breakfast, we walked a mile south to Punakaiki Pancake Rocks and Blowholes Park. This area of the West Coast has unique limestone rock formations that due to eons of erosion look like stacked rocks, hence the name, Pancake Rocks. The terrain lends itself for incoming seawater to shoot up huge geysers in-between the rocks. It really is quite fascinating to watch the water spray into the air and have the sunlight reveal a rainbow. We spent a few hours enjoying the scenery and then had lunch at a tourist bus stop — not the best place but we were hungry. We then wandered back along the driftwood-filled beach to the cottage. After a nap, we walked back to the tavern for a light dinner and then spent the rest of the evening talking with guests in the upstairs kitchen/dining room. What a wonderful view of the ocean and a great place to stay where the sunsets are magnificent.

I saw a lot of penguins in Antarctica

Jocelyn riding while I'm pushing

A beautiful scenic lunch spot

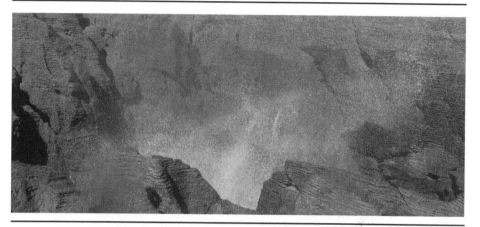

Punakaiki Pancake Rocks and Blowholes Park

Day 20: November 1st –
Punakaiki Beach to Greymouth

The early morning quickly turned to rain as we were getting ready to leave Punakaiki. We rigged for a wet ride and hoped it wouldn't rain too hard. The West Coast is known for torrential rains, and we didn't want to deal with that and traffic. The rain kept a steady pace as we rode out of town and into the rolling hills. The descents were a bit scary, as the brakes were wet and a few times I strayed too far into the oncoming lane on the curves. If an oncoming vehicle would have appeared, I doubt that stopping would have been possible. Sunshine or not, the coast was beautiful. We stopped in a small town of Runanga for a quick lunch and were surprised when Greymouth appeared so soon. It was only a 31 mile day, but the rain and coastal hills made it seem longer. We found a very cool and interesting hostel called Global Village Backpackers. I can't believe all the great accommodations we have stayed in. Each of these backpackers is so unique, and the international people are fun to mingle with. Global Village had an African theme throughout the inside and out.

The proprietor told us that Monteith's Brewery was a short five minute walk away. The previous night we had made reservations online for the 6:00 P.M. tour after meeting a guest at the Punakaiki backpacker who had started a new web site selling New Zealand adventures for a discount. We paid $6 for the brewery tour that is usually $20. The tour came with one tasting at the end and vouchers for three more glasses of your choice. Not bad for $6. Before that, there was time for a quick walk to the large local grocery store where we bought a plethora of fresh fruit and breakfast fixings. We really enjoyed the brewery tour and met a family from Wisconsin who were staying at Global Village. Since there was a restaurant inside the brewery, we decided to share a dinner of New Zealand green-lipped mussels and seafood chowder with our new friends. Inside the living room of Global Village, there were abundant mural world maps where we spent the evening talking with several guests about world travel while enjoying Monteith's beer and a roaring fire.

Tomorrow we will ride a short 30 miles to the next town of Hokitika. After that we will travel the 97 miles to Fox Glacier by bus, as there are several steep climbs on the narrow, winding mountain road to Franz Josef and Fox Glaciers. Along with that, the forecast called for continued rain the next few days. The West Coast was living up to its other name — "The Wet Coast".

Day 21: November 2nd – Greymouth to Hokitika

It started as another rainy day. We waited around to see what the weather was going to produce, so we didn't get on the road until after 10:00. Of course it started raining again and didn't let up, so it was a cold and rainy 30 mile ride to Hokitika. The first part of the ride was gravel on a "proper bike path" along the beach. After tiring of the bumpy road, we moved back to SH6 and soon arrived at another recommended backpackers called Birdsong. The proprietor from Global Village had made reservations for us the night before. There was a note and key on the office door that told us to make ourselves at home. I love these kinds of accommodations. We cleaned up and then called a taxi that took us the two miles into town for a little lunch and shopping. The taxi driver was a real hoot and super friendly. He told us of all the town highlights we needed to visit. I had planned to buy my wife Andee a unique piece of greenstone (jade), as Hokitika is the greenstone capital of New Zealand. After perusing several interesting shops and touring the cutting and polishing rooms, I decided on a store and a certain piece. After that, we stopped by a local pub for a pint and lunch. After a rude encounter with two locals who were well into their happy hour jugs for the afternoon, we decided to eat elsewhere. For some reason they didn't like bicyclists, and with our bike clothing and tattoos we did stand out. Another local came to our "rescue" and kicked them out. It was all pretty strange, as this was our first encounter with negative locals. We left, ate lunch elsewhere, and then stopped by a grocery store.

After that, Jocelyn called the taxi driver back for a pickup. When he asked if we had toured the town and we said no, he drove us around to show us the highlights. At the end he charged the same as when he had first brought us to town. A bicycle tour really is about the people. That evening we had another nice time chatting with guests in the very comfortable upstairs kitchen and dining room with a great beach view.

Tomorrow we will bus to Fox Glacier and hold out there until the weather clears for a hike or helicopter tour of the glaciers. I spent eight months walking on the ice in the Antarctic, but Jocelyn really wants to experience hiking on a glacier. The bus trip will also save a lot of time, as we have about 2 ½ weeks left before returning to Christchurch. There is still much to see and miles to cover, and I am now beginning to think my original route planning was a bit over enthusiastic. The South Island of New Zealand is a lot of territory to ride in six weeks.

Day 22-24: November 3rd-5th – Hokitika to Fox Glacier by Bus and Tourist Days

Last night, a full gale blew through and by Saturday morning the wind switched from the northeast to the southwest. Jocelyn was still sleeping, so I decided to light another fire in the living room and check my email. I received a message from Andee that my mother-in-law had passed away. She had suffered a few strokes in the past and had been ill. I called Andee and we talked for a while before I woke Jocelyn and gave her the phone. She took the news of her Grandma Polly passing very hard, as they had shared a special relationship. Jocelyn had talked with her before flying to New Zealand, but she wasn't well enough to talk. Jocelyn's uncle did say that she recognized her voice though. I asked Jocelyn what she wanted to do today, and she said, "Let's go, Dad."

The rain finally let up around 10:00 A.M., but the wind was still blowing hard for our two mile ride into downtown Hokitika. Since the bus wasn't scheduled to leave until 3:00 P.M., we spent several hours at the local library reading and snoozing. We had planned to ride around and explore the town, but the wind and rain changed our plans. Before riding to the bus stop, we found a nice cafe for lunch.

I have read and heard stories about how the InterCity Bus Lines doesn't like to take bikes, and we were no exception even though our reservations were made for 2 people and 2 bikes. We arrived at the bus stop and removed the panniers. The bus driver ignored us until I said we had reservations. He then went into a rant about how he had no notification on the manifest for bikes, and that was true because he showed us the manifest. So the bikes somehow had been dropped off the list. He went on and on about how there was no room until I looked inside, and there might have been 20 people on the 54 passenger bus. Then he said we had to completely take the bikes apart, so I just took the front wheels off and lowered the saddles so they would fit right in a baggage compartment that was totally empty. I guess he has had bad experiences with cyclists. I then paid him $20 for the bikes as the bus company said to pay the driver for the bikes. I guess it is a "tip" for him. Except for the two locals at a pub the previous afternoon giving us a hard time, this has been our only bad experience. Since we were upset about Grandma Polly, we weren't in much of a mood to deal with this driver. Jocelyn really had it out with him, so he finally quit complaining and did his job. We were really glad to take the bus, as the weather had deteriorated and the road past Franz Josef was very winding with steep hills and no shoulders.

The bus driver dropped us off at Ivory Towers Backpackers where we had reservations. We checked into a very small but inexpensive room and then set off to explore the town. There were a few businesses that advertised Fox Glacier hikes. We chose the one that advertised an ice climbing adventure. They also advertised helicopter rides to the top of the glacier that included a landing and hiking, but because of poor weather the helicopters hadn't been flying and were not expected to for a few more days. We made reservations for the ice climbing adventure for Monday morning since Sunday was booked. Back at Ivory Towers, we did our laundry and then found a nice restaurant for dinner. The family from Wisconsin that we'd met in Greymouth was also staying here, so we had another nice talk with them around the fireplace. It was then to bed after a long and tiring day.

On Sunday morning, we made breakfast and then hopped on our pannier-free bikes for a tour of the town and a trip to the glacier. This is the only glacier in the world that is fronted by a tropical rainforest. We rode through this forest along a long bicycle path before arriving at the glacier head. It was such a beautiful ride through giant ferns that eventually opened up to the sight of the huge Fox Glacier. We then parked our bikes and walked a trail to the beginning of the glacier walk. The weather was deteriorating quickly, so we returned to the bikes and Ivory Towers where we did our updates, read, and napped. The lazy afternoon passed quickly, and soon it was time for dinner at another restaurant.

That evening we made popcorn and shared a few beers as we sat with other guests in the large kitchen/dining room. There was a group of about 15 young blonde girls that caught my eye as they were cooking. In fact, I was staring at them until Jocelyn asked me what I was staring at. I replied,

"I have never seen such a large group of blonde girls." It was a sight to behold! I was really tempted to try and get a picture with them, but I chickened out and regret that now. I later learned from the manager that they were a Dutch group on an educational tour of New Zealand.

Monday morning dawned early, and we met our ice climbing instructor and were fitted with the proper clothes, boots, and gear. We were surprised that it was going to be just the two of us as students. Once at the glacier, we donned all the equipment and set out for our ice climbing adventure. Our guide was very friendly and informative as he gave us a history of the glacier. After a long hike, we came upon a cliff that was to be our first belayed drop and then climbing platform. Our instructor set up all the ropes and belaying lines and then told me to turn around and start walking down the cliff. We had never done this before, so telling me to "Walk off the edge" was very intimidating as my mind was telling me "No!" I eventually went over with my legs flailing; just what you are not supposed to do, while Jocelyn belayed me. Jocelyn did much better after seeing my mistakes. Once at the base of the 50 foot cliff, we explored a really cool recently discovered ice cave. Inside this blue ice cave were spirals where water had bored through to produce this cave.

Now it was time to climb. With a pick axe in each hand and ice climbing crampons on our boots, I attempted to start the 50 foot vertical climb. The procedure was to extend each axe as high as could be reached, stick the pick axe into the ice, and then repeat with the other pick. At this point one pulls himself up and sticks the toe spikes on the crampon into the face. It was the most physically challenging work I have ever done. After several slips that Jocelyn caught with the belaying line, I eventually made it to the top. The ice was very hard, so getting the pick axe and crampon spikes to stick were very difficult and resulted in lots of slipping. I then rappelled down the face, and Jocelyn and I changed positions for her turn. We worked several climbs including an inverted cliff face. Hanging upside down was very intimidating, but we did okay. After a quick lunch and lots of water we climbed out of the cave area and hiked up to what is called the "rapids" part of a glacier. It is comparable to extreme rapids on a rafting trip. Except on a glacier, this part is frozen and full of peaks and crevasses. At this point hiking is extremely difficult and dangerous. This was our turnaround point, so we hiked back along a different route and found lots of blue ice and clean refreshing glacier water to refill our water bottles with. We were soon done with the hike and bused back to the shop. After nine hours we were exhausted. Back at our room, we cleaned up and then visited a local bar that was recommended. After enjoying a few beers while sitting in front of the huge fireplace, we were finally rested and warm enough to eat a meal. At Ivory Towers we prepared to get on the road again. Haast Pass, a very difficult steep climb, was coming soon. But first the town of Haast was 70 miles away with questionable accommodations along the way. Once again, 70 miles on our cross-country Southern Tier route was the norm, but 70 miles in New Zealand is a pretty challenging day.

A tropical rainforest in front of Fox Glacier

Ice climbing on Fox Glacier

Day 25: November 6th –
Fox Glacier to Haast Junction

The morning started out drizzling as we rode out of the tropical rainforest of Fox Glacier and headed south. The ride through huge fern plants was very pretty and inspirational. Since SH6 doesn't have any shoulders in this area, we were happy that there was very little traffic on this Tuesday morning. We met the driftwood-filled beach at Bruce Bay that led to the Tasman Sea. The sandflies kept us going even though we wanted to explore the beach. The first possible accommodation was 42 miles at Lake Paringa, but we kept moving as we didn't see anywhere inviting to stay. Around lunchtime we spotted a sign for South Westland Salmon Farm Restaurant that seemed like it was in the "middle of nowhere".

After a delicious lunch of salmon, we decided to push the 30 miles into Haast even if there were accommodations along the way. We were soon on the shore of the large and beautiful Lake Motaki before encountering the coastal three large hills climb before Haast. We powered through the peak of the largest hill at Knight's Point where we stopped at a rest stop and enjoyed the beautiful bay view. After the last hill, it was a ten mile flat speed run to Haast. At this point, Jocelyn had caught a second wind and was way ahead. At a ranch to our right, I noticed a herd of cows running every which way as they were being chased by a pickup and several dogs. All of a sudden they turned and were running back toward me. The ranch hand was having a tough time herding these cows. I later learned that they were chasing after Jocelyn who then turned around to see where I was. I imagine the ranch hand was a little perturbed that his cows were being "herded" by a cyclist. It was pretty funny watching though!

We finally arrived at a nice motel in Haast after ten hours on the road. We knew there was a local backpacker but were too tired to find it. Next door was a quick mart where we saw a cyclist couple who also looked like they had been riding all day, probably from Haast Pass. At the checkout we grunted hellos to each other as neither of us felt like talking. They were purchasing milk and bread while we had a six pack of beer, ice cream, and chips. I think we enjoyed ourselves more that evening!

"Difficulties are just things to overcome." – Ernest Shackleton

Day 26: November 7th – Haast Junction to Makarora

Last night we had a good dinner at the one and only pub, followed by a good rest. We knew Haast Pass that connects the West Coast with the Central Otago Valley was known as a very steep and difficult climb because we were going the "wrong way". The peak is less than 1,800 feet, but this climb is only for about 4 miles. The first 25 miles were fairly easy with the usual ups and downs, but then the steep climbing started. The views were just amazing, and this ride is known as one of the most beautiful in all of New Zealand. Riding through a rainforest along the Haast River surrounded by snowcapped mountains with a waterfall around every curve was just awesome. This has got to be one of the most beautiful rides in the world with tree canopies covering the road. The challenge of the climb just made it more awesome. The climbing soon turned into an occasional walk, and the true meaning of what Kiwis call a "push bike" came through. We have climbed higher but not as steep.

Soon we reached the peak and screamed down the other side. What a trip! Otago Valley was equally beautiful, and we found a nice A-frame cabin in the tiny town of Makarora. I did the laundry and hung it out to dry while Jocelyn sunbathed and napped. I then went into the lodge bar to update my website and enjoy a few beers. Jocelyn soon found me, and we enjoyed a delicious Italian dinner with the three other guests. Our only neighbors were a small herd of sheep that didn't seem to care that we were close to them. The cabin was very comfortable and we enjoyed a long rest.

A warm, sunny day after descending Haast Pass

Day 27: November 8ᵗʰ – Makarora to Lake Wanaka

After a quiet morning I went to checkout at the lodge office, when the clerk asked me what I thought of the election. After a few moments of gathering my thoughts, I remembered that the presidential election had been yesterday, and I replied, "Who won?"

At this point the clerk was baffled with my response and said, "Obama." At which I responded, "Oh," and turned around and left. I'm sure he was wondering what kind of an American I was. Unless there was a nearby television (and Makarora didn't have TV or cell phone service), we never made it a point to check news online.

Quote of the day from Jocelyn: "We are never going to get anywhere if you keep stopping and taking pictures, Dad." It was a post card day as we cycled along Lake Wanaka, passed The Neck, which separates the two lakes, and then Lake Hawea. We could not have asked for nicer weather with the sun shining bright and no wind at all. The lake water was bright blue, and with the surrounding mountains the views were absolutely stunning as we glanced down at the crystal-clear water. The lakeshore ride lasted about 30 wonderful miles. One of the things that really stood out was that there are no homes at all around the lakes except at a small resort town at the southern end of Lake Hawea, and we only saw one boat.

At one of the lake lookouts, we ran into a group from Switzerland that we had talked with at the backpacker where we stayed at Fox Glacier a few nights earlier. Like one of the guys said, "It's a small island."

As we were riding up a last hill into Wanaka, I fell for the first time. I have been run off the road twice before but managed to stay upright. On this, the shoulder-less climb, a car came way too close so I moved a bit to the left and wound up sliding down a small embankment in the gravel. Falling on a bike isn't good, but loaded down with panniers makes it worse. People in a truck that saw it happen immediately stopped to help. I recovered, and since it was only a few more miles to our backpacker for the night, we pressed on with my twisted and very sore back.

We found Wanakabakpaka on a beautiful spot overlooking the southern end of Lake Wanaka. We learned of a Mexican restaurant in town and it was really good. Those of you who have read our first journal of crossing the U.S. know that we crossed the country eating Mexican food. In fact, we crossed Texas one taco at a time! After dinner, we explored the very pretty town and harbor area where there was a sailboat race on the lake. That evening, we met more guests and enjoyed a bottle of wine while looking out the huge living room window at the lake.

'The Neck' between Lakes Wanaka and Hawea

Overlooking Lake Hawea

Day 28: November 9th –
Lake Wanaka to Queenstown

I spent a sleepless night in bed trying to get comfortable with my sore back. Yesterday's fall produced a lower back pain that had me getting up several times to try and walk it out. By the time Jocelyn woke up, I knew we wouldn't be riding to the top of the 3,500 foot Crown Saddle even though it was one of the rides I was really looking forward to. After wandering around and talking with locals, I found a guy to take us up to the top, figuring we could then ride down the other side into Queenstown. This was a huge help, as we really wanted to be in Queenstown today for a few days rest for non-riding activities.

On the drive to the Crown Saddle, we stopped at the cyclist famous Cardrona Hotel, a pub built in 1863. What a fantastic place to step back in time, and I have seen it on so many biking blogs. It was 11:00 A.M. but a perfect time for a pint of Cardrona's local brew. After that, we were soon at the top and started our exhilarating ride down the mountain, as the ride to the top is a low-grade rise to 3,500 feet over 24 miles, but the other side is very steep and drops to 1,200 feet in about 6 miles. As I worked the brakes, I continued to cringe with the scary fast descent through the European-style switchbacks. I have never gone so fast on a bike and continued to stare at the road and hold tight. The 55 plus pounds of baggage on each bike didn't help. Every time I strayed into the oncoming lane, I was thankful there were no cars there. Once the descent was complete, the ups and downs to Queenstown became painful, but I knew there would be rest at the end.

The road was very busy, but fortunately we spied a lakeside bike path that although gravel and dirt was very inviting. After several miles along the lake, we were soon in downtown Queenstown and the GPS found our way up a very steep hill to the Butterfli (spelled correctly) Lodge. The view from this backpacker of Queenstown Bay and the surrounding ski slope gondola and hills is beautiful. It was a quick ten-minute walk to downtown where there is everything and anything to do, as Queenstown is known for adventure. There were outdoor shops galore along with many businesses selling adventure trips of all types, whether it is on the water, air, or land. We found a nice restaurant on the bay and enjoyed delicious oysters and scallops. Then we made our way to the local grocery store where we stocked up for a few days.

Back at the Butterfli Lodge, we made ourselves at home and started a fire while enjoying a bottle of local wine. As we sat at the main dining room table while other guests cooked, we talked with two Dutch girls touring New Zealand and an older gentleman from England who was visiting his brother after selling his bowling business in England. We chatted with them for over three hours. Staying in these hostels is like owning a big home where all these strangers come in and cook and talk with you and then clean up and leave.

The top of Crown Saddle with Queenstown
off in the distance between us.

A steep descent toward Queenstown

We found a nice lakeside bike path that routed us past downtown

Days 29-31: November 10th-12th – Tourist Days in Queenstown

We spent a long weekend in Queenstown, hiking, exploring, and partaking in a few adventures. Since it was a weekend, the town was packed with tourists on crowded streets, restaurants, and bars. All of the surrounding hotels were also packed with buses. It was quite overwhelming to us. Jocelyn decided that she wanted to bungee jump, and what better place to live this adventure then in Queenstown, the birth of the bungee jump. And, of course, she didn't want to jump at the more popular venues but wanted the big experience of the largest jump in New Zealand, the Nevis Gorge, a massive 440 foot 8.5 second drop! Since the weather wasn't looking good for Sunday, we signed up for an early Saturday trip, with me as a spectator, and rode 45 minutes out of town on the Nevis Gorge bus. The Nevis Gorge was spectacular as we rode a small cable trolley to the middle jumping platform. Jocelyn volunteered to jump first, and there was a big lump in my throat as she performed a perfect dive off the platform attached to a thick rubber bungee. When she was raised back onto the platform, she wanted to jump again but there were a few others in line. She described the experience as totally awesome and wondered why her dad didn't want to jump as I might have jumped at a smaller venue. Just being a spectator connected to the platform with a harness was enough for me. All of this adventure was captured on video and pictures through the business – a perfect souvenir! Back in town, we found a Mexican restaurant to celebrate with a few beers and another great meal.

Our original plan was to cycle the 180 miles to Milford Sound and then start the return to Christchurch. With time running out and with very limited non-camping accommodations at Milford Sound and along the way, we were hesitant to start that trip. A rock slide outside the Homer Tunnel and only entrance to Milford Sound sealed the fate of that ride. The road was closed, so the only access was by air. On Saturday afternoon, we researched the variety of airline companies that flew to Milford Sound.

The manager of the hostel was very familiar with one of the companies, and after more research we let her book our flight. The weather did not look good for Sunday, so we decided to stay in Queenstown an extra day and booked the flight for Monday. We spent Sunday hiking, working on the bikes, and napping. We were both tired of the "adventure town" atmosphere and ready to roll.

We did one more "adventurous" activity on Sunday. After our cross-country ride, we'd both had a tattoo inked on our left calves of an outline of the U.S. with a bicycle inside. This was a memorial to our Southern Tier crossing in 2011. We had talked about another tattoo to memorialize this trip. As we were walking through town, we came upon a tattoo parlor and decided to check out a possible design. We told the tattoo artist that we wanted a tattoo of New Zealand next to our U.S. one but that we wanted a bicycle theme in the outline. He drew a cool sketch of a bicycle gear inside the South and North islands of the country. We were both immediately impressed by his drawing and returned in an hour for the work. I never thought I would get another tattoo, but this one worked out well too. Now we have two tattoos memorializing our bicycle journeys.

Our New Zealand time was running short, so we discussed our next move. Riding the 775 miles from Queenstown to Christchurch seemed out of the question, as that would take about 12 days and there are few accommodations along the way for the first major part of the distance. We were also scheduled on a November 25th flight to Sydney, Australia. The other choice was to ride the Otago Rail Trail, a 90 mile gravel bike trail converted from an old railroad line. We had heard from several people that this trail is a must ride in New Zealand. The Otago Rail Trail can be ridden in two days, but to really enjoy and encounter the several varied parts of central New Zealand it was recommended to spend four days exploring this trail. We decided on the Otago Rail Trail, and the next decision was to ride it from the West to the East Coast or vice-versa. We could cycle the 50 miles to the west railhead in the town of Clyde and then ride the trail to Dunedin and then take a bus north for the return to Christchurch. I have read that the return up SH1 to Christchurch is very boring and busy with not much to see. On the other hand, the bus ride up the central part of the South Island passes by the beautiful glacier lakes of Tekapo and Pukaki with views of Mt. Cook, the highest mountain in New Zealand. We decided to ride the trail from the east to the west, which meant we could either ride the 175 miles to Dunedin from Queenstown or bus it. In the interest of time, we decided to take the bus to Dunedin, so we purchased the tickets for Tuesday.

Monday dawned a beautiful day, and our pilot picked us up for our Milford Sound adventure. I did not realize that we were to be the only passengers and the plane was a four seat Cessna. The business ad showed a larger plane, but since we were the only early-morning customers, we were in for a real treat on our private excursion. The ride over the mountains was totally awesome, as our pilot pointed out several areas where "The Lord of the Rings" was filmed. Jocelyn sat in the front and took picture after picture while I was in back doing the same. Several times she turned around and looked at me with a huge smile. We could not believe the immense beauty of the snow-covered mountains from the air. We landed, or "crabbed in", at the Milford Sound airport since the wind was blowing hard sideways. A short walk later, we were at the boat dock for a water excursion out to the Tasman Sea and back along the sound. Milford Sound was formed thousands of years ago by many glaciers that carved this very deep sound surrounded by huge cliffs. The boat excursion was fun, as the captain edged the nose into a huge waterfall. We were prepared for this, and our jackets were drenched by the cold, fresh water. It seemed like everywhere you looked there was a waterfall. As the trip continued, we ate lunch onboard while enjoying the many seals and penguins swimming through the sound. All too soon, the boat trip ended and we found our pilot waiting for us. We walked back to the airport and were soon airborne again for a different spectacular route back to Queenstown. We will forever remember this awesome plane ride. The time spent in Queenstown was fun but twice as long as we expected due to the weather. But we were rewarded with two adventures of a lifetime, the Nevis Gorge bungee jump and the wonderful sightseeing flight and cruise on Milford Sound.

Milford Sound

Beautiful aerial scenery

Ready to jump!

A perfect dive

A 440 foot 8.5 second drop!

Day 32: November 13th –
Bus from Queenstown to Dunedin

We packed, loaded the bikes, and rode the few miles through downtown to the bus stop. We were anxious about how much of a hassle the bus driver was going to be with our bikes. As we were waiting for the bus, I saw two friends of mine from McMurdo on the ice walk by, so we had a nice chat with them. They had just returned from the Milford Sound hike and were back in town for some sightseeing. It truly is a small island. A small bus drove up, and we thought our bikes would never fit. But the driver was very friendly, noted our reservations for two bikes, and quickly loaded them in the back luggage compartment followed by our panniers. At that point, the compartment was pretty full. The trip to Dunedin was about four hours with a quick lunch stop.

We disembarked from the bus at the Taieri Gorge Railway Station near downtown Dunedin. I went inside the station and purchased two tickets for the train ride to Pukerangi, which is the last stop before the east railhead town of Middlemarch. Bikes travel free. We had reservations at a downtown backpackers but had a difficult time finding it with our GPS. I think that riding in another large town was pretty confusing as there was lots of traffic and streets. The last several weeks have been spent in small towns and off the major roads, so this was quite disorientating. We eventually found it on a side street and carried our bikes and panniers up narrow stairs and into a small noisy room next to the kitchen/dining area. It wasn't a very nice place, and the old bathrooms were all the way on the other side. But we only needed a place to sleep as the train was scheduled to leave early the next morning.

While perusing the lobby area, I noticed an advertisement for Speight's Brewery Tour in the downtown area. I asked the clerk for directions and was told it was a ten minute walk away. It didn't take much to talk Jocelyn into this, so we were off. Speight's Beer is one of my favorite New Zealand beers, and this seemed like a real treat. The tour was excellent and informative and actually included a history of beer along with a history of

New Zealand and Dunedin. After the tour, we were lead into the tasting room where there were six flavors on tap. Our guide told us we had 30 minutes to taste all we wanted, and since there were only eight people, we had an outstanding time! Since we were walking, we readily indulged in all the flavors.

As we walked back to the hostel, we stopped at a really nice pizza pub and sat outside in the setting sun to enjoy an excellent vegetarian pizza. That evening, we sat in the living/TV room and worked on our website updates and enjoyed a few shows.

Day 33: November 14th – Train from Dunedin to Pukerangi

We checked out early and rode the few miles back to the train station where we removed the panniers and handed our bikes up to the porter in the luggage car. We then found our passenger car and settled into our comfortable seats. I like trains so I was really looking forward to this. We could have cycled to the railhead in Middlemarch, but everywhere I read said this train trip was the easy, fun, and scenic way to go. Our breakfast consisted of an egg-salad sandwich, chips, and a small bottle of wine which we enjoyed as the countryside rolled by. What a nice break! The train rode along a deep gorge that at times seemed directly next to us. After 2 ½ hours, we rolled to a stop at Pukerangi Station which is marked by only a sign. We disembarked and retrieved our bikes and panniers and the train reversed itself for the return to Dunedin. The actual start of the Otago Rail Trail is in the town of Middlemarch, another 15 miles down a gravel road. Waiting at the Pukerangi Station were a few cars and vans to take guests to various hotels along the trail or to the Middlemarch bike shop for a bicycle rental. The proprietor of this bike shop saw us and offered to transport our panniers to his shop because it is a pretty rough, gravelly ride with all our weight. We readily agreed to this, and we rode off without our panniers.

It was a fun, hilly, and wide-open valley ride to Middlemarch. Without our panniers, we were racing along even on the gravel, and the freedom from the panniers was a needed break. We were soon in Middlemarch, picked up our panniers from the bike shop, and proceeded to the recommended lodging at the local pub. The pub had a very clean and nice accommodation that we thoroughly enjoyed. We explored the small town and then spent our evening in the pub talking with the locals and enjoying a few pints with a delicious fish dinner. It was soon time for bed, and we were anxious to explore the Otago Rail Trail.

Day 34: November 15th – Middlemarch to Ranfurly

We had an early start on the trail where it soon started raining. We continued through the muddy trail and gave greetings to many cyclists headed the opposite way. The countryside was beautiful especially with the low-elevation snow on the surrounding mountains. Our speed was slowed considerably due to the loose gravel and rain. Lunchtime finally came five hours later at the Waipiata Tavern where we enjoyed a pint and a delicious, warming soup. The rail trail is also known as the "Ale Trail" and this was the first of many pubs along the way. When we left, I discovered my second puncture, probably from a sharp stone as I couldn't find anything on the tire. After fixing that, we rode a quick 10 km to the town of Ranfurly where we found the Post Office Backpackers. This hostel was converted from an old post office many years ago and has several rooms added to a main house. The proprietor was very friendly and informative of Ranfurly and told us that we were quite early for the biking season so we were the only guests. For dinner he recommended a local sports pub where we enjoyed another good fish dinner. The evening was spent reading by the huge fireplace. There was no heat in the main building so I kept the fire going all night.

The start of the Central Otago Rail Trail

One of the many old train tunnels we rode through

A beautiful day on the trail

Day 35: November 16ᵗʰ – Ranfurly to Omakau

This morning, I cooked a big breakfast and kept the fire going. It felt strange to be in this huge building by ourselves, so we took our time as overnight the wind had picked up considerably and it was very cold. We rejoined the still muddy trail with the rain threatening again and were greeted by many horses, sheep, and cows. There were several sheep that had escaped the fences and were running along the trail. Some were more used to humans than others and just stared at us. The views were completely different than yesterday as we have ridden through forests, flat farming areas, and desert-like stretches. We pretty much experienced it all on the Otago Rail Trail with gentle climbing, a nice break for us. We rode through several old train tunnels that were built in 1890. These tunnels were very narrow, and both ends were adorned with curved ornamental bricks. We stopped at a trailside café in Lauder for a delicious gourmet lunch before continuing on a few more miles to Omakau. As we neared the main street, we heard two ladies who had just started an afternoon bike ride on the trail say to us, "It's too windy, so we are going back to town for an ice cream." We were still fighting the headwind while they were riding with it. While riding through the small town of Omakau, we came upon the 100 year-old Hotel Omakau. Since there were rooms available and there was only one other accommodation in town, we decided to stay in this very historic hotel. The bikes were left in a shed, so we hauled all our panniers up to a small room on the second floor. The pub turned out to be the town's gathering place, so we enjoyed conversation, pints, and dinner with the locals. Everyone was telling us about a major storm heading this way and to sit tight tomorrow because the trail can get very windswept with thunderstorms. After a very entertaining evening, we retired to our room thinking we might be staying another night.

The trains must have been smaller then

Much different scenery than when we started our tour, but still beautiful

Day 36: November 17ᵗʰ – A Weather Hold in Omakau

That night, thunderstorms rolled in on a constant wave. At daybreak, the rain was pouring down as a weather front from the Tasman Sea swept through the South Island. The temperature continued to drop, so we decided to spend another night but the Hotel Omakau was booked for a large birthday celebration this Saturday night. I walked two doors down to the only other accommodation in town, and fortunately there was one room available. We moved our bikes and panniers in the pouring rain to our new accommodation and settled in for the long day. We were comfortable as we read, napped, and did laundry. Occasionally, the rain would let up and we would take a quick walk and see several cyclists struggling through town as this was a Saturday which is a popular trail day. We were happy to have the luxury of time on our side and to not be riding another muddy, wet trail day. That evening, we once again ate at the Hotel Omakau pub and also enjoyed the birthday festivities that had spilled out of the courtyard barbeque area into the pub. Several people gave us a forecast of a nice day tomorrow.

Peace on the trail

Day 37: November 18ᵗʰ – Omakau to Cromwell

Sunday morning was clear but very windy and cold. The local hills had received a dusting of snow and it was very pretty to ride with this view. Except for the strong headwinds and cold, it was a very pleasant ride. We stopped at the "i Site" (New Zealand's Visitor Information Centers) in Alexandra to change our bus reservations to Christchurch. We had reservations from Alexandra (near the trail end) but decided to make our last stop 20 miles north in Cromwell as the weather had turned warm and pleasant. We can't say enough about these Visitor Information Centers as they are so friendly and offer bookings, maps, publications, and a wealth of local knowledge. I had purchased several $9 maps of the South Island but could have gotten by with the free ones. After our brief stop, we continued to our end of the trail at the railhead in Clyde. This is the usual beginning of the trail for most riders. In fact, we never saw anyone on the trail heading in our direction. We chose to ride from east to west as we wanted our Christchurch return through the interior past the glacier lakes of Pukaki and Tekapo along with Mt. Cook.

We put on our climbing legs one last time as we rode alongside the beautiful Cromwell Gorge. There was very little traffic, and we were soon in the small town of Cromwell on Lake Dunstan. We found the only backpackers in town – "The Pinot Lodge". Once we were settled in our room, we walked downtown to the local pub for a light late lunch. We were both pretty quiet and reflective, thinking about the end of our New Zealand Adventure. I was anxious to return home since I had left in early February, but we both still wanted to ride more. We shopped at the grocery store, returned to the lodge, cooked dinner, and then retired early. Tomorrow we return to Christchurch by a 7 hour bus trip. Our last cycle ride will be to navigate through Christchurch tomorrow to Natural High Adventure Cycles and return the bikes. I had hoped our Christchurch return would be up the interior on our cycles, but time is short. We will spend a few days in Christchurch before flying to Sydney for a five day stay at Bondi Beach. We hope the surf is good and the water warmer than New Zealand. We will then return to Florida.

The end of the trail

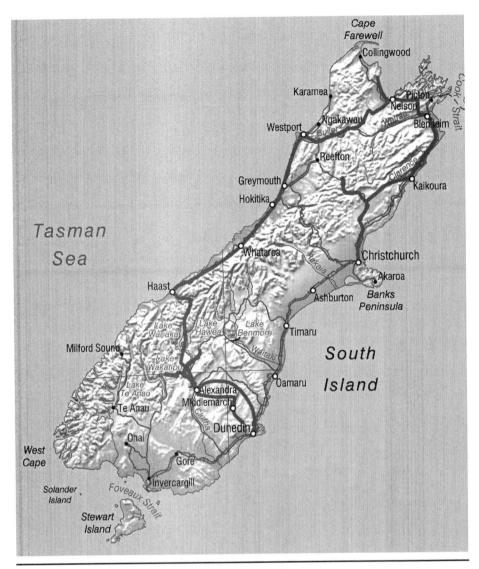

Our New Zealand cycling route

Day 38: November 19ᵗʰ – Bus from Cromwell to Christchurch

We had another lazy morning as the bus didn't leave until 3:00. At noon, we packed up and toured around town and the Lake Dunstan areas. After a nice lunch in the older part of town, we rode to the bus stop where we soon boarded a small bus. Once again, the Atomic Shuttle driver was very courteous and had no problem loading our bikes. As we rode the 255 miles to Christchurch over the Lindis Pass, there were no towns or accommodations until Omarama (67 miles), so camping gear would have been a must on this stretch. We will save this long cycle ride for another day. The shuttle driver stopped at Lake Pukaki for a wonderful view of the lake with Mt. Cook in the background. At 11,262 feet, Mt. Cook is the tallest mountain in New Zealand. We continued on to Lake Tekapo. These glacier lakes have such a bright color to them, and I have never seen such blue water before. It was after 11:00 P.M. when we reached our Christchurch destination of Jailhouse Backpackers. This backpacker was a real jail that was built in 1874. Our room key was waiting on the front desk. Even though it was late, we sat up and enjoyed a few glasses of wine as we talked about our awesome journey.

Day 39: November 20ᵗʰ – We Have Reached the End of Another Adventure

Tuesday morning found us navigating through downtown Christchurch rush hour to return the bikes to Natural High. Without family and friends to greet us, it was pretty anticlimactic. Jeremy removed our equipment from the bikes, and then we took a taxi ride to the U.S. Antarctic Center where I picked up a duffel bag I had stored. After that, it was back to the Jailhouse where we packed two duffel bags full of bike gear and then took another taxi to a local post office for mailing back to Florida. Then it was on to a grocery store and back to the Jailhouse. What a long and successful end of our journey!

Last year, when we crossed America from Florida to California, I never would have thought that the following year we would be cycle touring New Zealand. Thanks to my Antarctic adventure for leading us to this destination. It has been a trip with many difficult but rewarding rides. From reading many biking blogs, I knew the hills and weather would be challenging, but I never imagined to what extent. At times the everyday climbing seemed insurmountable, but with the right attitude we took each hill and mountain foot by foot. There was new meaning to the Kiwi term of calling a bicycle a "push bike", as there were times when we literally pushed our bikes over a steep hill or mountain. We'd spent over two hours pushing our bikes to the top of the very steep Haast Pass. Several people commented that we biked the "wrong way" over the pass. But we survived foot by foot and the rise seemed endless at the time. Our highest climb was over 3,900 feet over the course of several hours, so we were able to stay on the saddle. Overall, our total ascent was over 38,000 feet. That is a lot of "ups and downs"!

I never would have imagined us cycling in near hurricane-force winds, but we did, although sometimes we had to walk the bikes to stay out of the road. The windy passes made for some exhilarating descents, although peddling hard to get down a steep hill was sometimes demoralizing, as the reward for climbing a steep hill is the so-called easy descent. There were several times we had to do this. The tales of heavy rain on the West (aka "Wet") Coast didn't disappoint, and with the proper rain gear we survived. The sandflies really were not in "bloom" yet, so we survived those okay except that Jocelyn was affected more than I was. We were prepared with mosquito netting but never used it.

The weather was kind to us, except that we would have enjoyed it being warmer. All the locals who we talked to said it was very unseasonable and that the cooler weather would normally have passed by now as New Zealand is well into spring. It was cool or cold in most areas, and we couldn't imagine camping on the cold ground. Because of that and the weight of all the gear, we'd mailed the hired camping gear back to Christchurch after our first climb into Hanmer Springs. While there, we experienced our first backpackers (hostel) and figured this would be a fun and affordable alternative.

My observations:

Weather: October and November should have been warmer. The rain was kind to us, but the wind was very challenging as we expected.

Hills: A lot more than what I expected. As a result, our daily mileage was much less than planned. I was okay with that, and to see all that we wanted we made up time with four bus trips.

Riding days: Less than expected, as we took more time off to do tourist stuff. Once again I was okay with that as we wanted to experience New Zealand and not just ride around the South Island. We had the bikes a total of 39 days.

Actual riding days: 27

Sightseeing days: 8

Bad weather days: 4

The people: I can't say enough about how much we enjoyed talking with and living among the New Zealand people. Except for a few rare times, we felt very comfortable with their kindness and generosity. I never hesitated to ask for help or directions, although you should never try to out drink a Kiwi at the local pub, as it just won't happen.

Favorite town: Wanaka, which is such a pretty and laid-back lakeside community. Along with that, it has a really cool sailing scene.

Our bicycles: I rode a Specialized Sirrus Touring Bike that was comfortable and performed well in all areas except climbing. Jocelyn rode a Cannondale Touring T2 which was equipped with an extra gear at 27 speeds. While I was walking, she would still be riding. She did have problems with brake adjustments, but other than that it suited her well as she rides a Surly Long Haul Trucker at home. Two other touring riders we talked with had 30 speeds with climbing gears. They said they still had to walk some of the hills. One couple from Montana only paid the airlines $75 each way for their bikes, while a Canadian couple said they paid $200 each way. It was easy to hire the bikes and drop them off when done. Natural High Adventure Cycles in Christchurch was really a smart choice for hiring the bikes. Andy, Sandra, and Jeremy were very knowledgeable, kind, and helpful.

Our trip: Originally I had planned a 42 day, 2,000 mile ride around most of the South Island. As I have said, early on I knew that wasn't going to happen. We instead covered all of the planned areas except for one, Picton and Queen Charlotte Sound in the north, as we wanted to spend more time at Able Tasman National Park and the West Coast. We were able to cover all the areas by utilizing a shuttle bus four times. We bussed from Blenheim to Nelson (72 miles), Hokitika to Fox Glacier (97 miles), Queenstown to Dunedin (175 miles), and Cromwell to Christchurch (255 miles). The bus total is about 600 miles. This is interesting, because if you add our total riding miles of around 1,100 to the bus miles of 600, it is close to the planned 2,000 miles. Without utilizing the bus, we would have missed large areas. Also, we had originally planned to ride the 180 miles from Queenstown to Milford Sound and then bus out, so that puts it pretty close to the 2,000 miles. As it turned out, we rode some of the best rides New Zealand has to offer.

Bus companies: We used three companies. InterCity Bus Line is not bicycle friendly at all. A bicycle space cannot be reserved, so whether the bike can be taken on the bus is at the whim of the driver. We not only experienced this but also heard the same thing from other riders. We also hired Atomic Shuttle and Connexions Bus. Both of these will accept bike reservations and are very biker friendly.

Accommodations: We spent almost every night in a backpacker (hostel) and were always able to obtain a twin private room with shared toilet/shower facilities. When one wasn't available, we stayed in a motel or campground that was equipped with cabins, as most are. The backpackers are fun and affordable. They are like staying in a different house every night. Most have fireplaces or wood-burning heaters which I serviced most happily as I really missed my fireplace at home. None of them had a propane gas-assisted start like mine at home, so my fire starting skills increased. We would eat out, or if a grocery store were nearby we would shop and cook. The dinner scene at these backpackers can be very fun and enlightening with many different nationalities "cooking up a storm" at once. We just had to get in there and get it done sometimes! I have always been a pretty quiet guy, but I really enjoyed talking with so many different people.

The roads: For the most part, all the roads we traveled on were in good condition although a wider shoulder would have been nice. To the left of the white line it quickly became loose gravel. The Otago Rail Trail was all gravel with varying degrees of gravel size and distribution. It was very muddy and wavering one day. We could ride abreast or in a single lane as there are no vehicles allowed. There were other bikers, hikers, and horses.

Drivers: Once again, for the most part the drivers were very courteous and gave us wide berth since there was little or no shoulder for most of the South Island. The dairy truck drivers are very fast and do not like to move over even if there is no oncoming traffic. I was run off the road three times, twice by trucks. Fortunately, I only fell once on an uphill road to Wanaka. After a few days rest in Queenstown I was fine. The tourist's crazy driving in their campervans that I had read about never happened. Maybe it was because the season hadn't really started yet. We never rode on a motorway and pretty much kept off of the major roads except for the West Coast where the only way up or down is on SH6.

Hitchhiking: We did manage to hitch short rides twice, once when it was getting late on the way to Kaikoura and there were no accommodations and again when I hurt my back when I fell.

Food: While in the Antarctic for the winter, I had changed my eating habits to vegetarian and pretty much stayed that way in New Zealand. Jocelyn decided to go with that diet also. After a few weeks of seeing "bangers and mash" on the pub menus, I really wanted to try it. So I did and it was delicious, but I haven't touched meat since. We ate lots of excellent grilled and baked fish, fish and chips, seafood chowders, scallops and mussels, salads, vegetarian quiches, and nachos. And of course we ate whatever we wanted because we were burning calories.

Favorite ride: There were so many great scenic vistas, but my favorite was after the town of Charleston on the West Coast. We climbed three steep hills with each hill having several peaks. After the last one, we were totally exhausted and even the fast downhill descent was hurting with the headwinds. But soon we were on the coast to one of the most fantastic scenes I have ever cycled in, as the West Coast revealed beautiful palm trees and a rock-bound coast with crashing waves. I thought we had ridden into Jurassic Park! We stopped many times and just marveled at the beauty and power.

Beer and Wine: The huge variety of small and large operations is amazing. We toured two breweries along with several winery tastings. We had so many different types and flavors of both. One of our favorites was any beer from Monteith's Brewery in Greymouth. When we were really thirsty, we stuck with several flavors of Speight's beer. The Central Otago Pinot Noirs were also great.

Food: Very expensive!

Father and Daughter: Once again we did well together. Jocelyn kept me on the left side of the road when I strayed. It didn't take long getting used to the other side of the road, but some mornings I got on the wrong side. She watched over me. Last year she was usually in the lead, but this time I was at point. I knew it was time for a break when she gave me the look or was quiet all of a sudden. We had good times together, but occasionally we needed our own space and were sometimes spread apart. Some of the rides were talkative and some were plain quiet as we absorbed the beauty. At times, one of us would just stop and would not start again until we were ready. The other knew to just wait. It was really good that we could talk to other people in the backpackers. But through it all, we never complained of the daily routine of getting back on the road. It became second nature and we greeted each morning as a new day of discovery.

The locals: The cows, sheep, bulls, llamas, deer, horses, pigs, and dogs were everywhere and I enjoyed stopping to watch them. What is interesting is that we were never chased by a dog even though there were many on the loose.

This map of the South Island says it all

The end of our New Zealand adventure

Epilogue

I would like to once again thank my wife Andee for her understanding with this adventure. In the past 27 months, I have only been home for two. I would also like to thank my son Cary for looking after things at the house and helping his mom out.

And once again I would like to thank Jocelyn for being my traveling buddy. We did it again and had fun exploring together! While spending the winter of 2012 at McMurdo Station, Antarctic, I wrote Part One about our cross-country adventure. During the winter of 2013 in the South Pole, I have completed New Zealand Part Two of this book.

In June, Jocelyn and a friend completed the TransAmerica Bicycle Trail from Virginia Beach to Washington State. They cycled the grand American adventure of over 3,000 miles.

Jocelyn and Rachel at the completion of the
TransAmerica Bicycle Journey

"The Pole...Great God! this is an awful place and terrible enough for us to have laboured to it without the reward of priority. Well, it is something to have got here, and the wind may be our friend to-morrow. Now for the run home and a desperate struggle. I wonder if we can do it."

— Captain Robert Falcon Scott

These are the words of Captain Robert Falcon Scott when he and the other four in his expedition arrived at the South Pole in January 1912, one month after Norwegian explorer Roald Amundsen. Scott and his party were facing an 800 mile return to the coast. Today, we have the luxury of a quick three hour flight aboard a ski-equipped LC-130 Hercules.

Closing Words on my Antarctic Adventures

We recently celebrated an Antarctic Midwinter which is a continent-wide celebration during the Austral Winter Solstice. Last year in McMurdo at a special midwinter's dinner, this toast was made by Harry House:

McMurdo Mid-winter Dinner 2012 – by Harry House

Mid-winter day is a time of great significance here in the Antarctic. Celestially, it is defined as the shortest 'day' of the year and the beginning of the Sun's gradual return in August. Early explorers would mark the day with feasts and commemorative toasts to loved ones back home. For them, the day provided a much-needed morale boost after many months of isolation. It marked a 'pivot point' whereby they could start anticipating a call to action in the gathering dawn.

Much has changed since the Heroic Age of Antarctic exploration, both on the ice and back 'in the world'. There are no Poles to discover any longer (although there are other things). Nations no longer wait breathlessly in anticipation of our safe return, carrying word of feats of endurance and discovery. We can converse with our loved ones back home in almost real time, so our feeling of isolation is much reduced from the days of yore. Certainly we now enjoy many of the comforts of home by comparison, although at times we all lose sight of that. It is easy and reasonable in many ways for us to feel our contributions pale in comparison to the legends of the past. It is understandable that many of us no longer feel any connection to those who came before us, or even to the legacy of the Continent of Antarctica.

While all of this may be true, it misses the point. Having the privilege of working here in the winter is still one of the most unique opportunities in the world. For that reason alone we are all now members of an exclusive group of individuals who share a common bond. This bond extends not only with each other, but across all the stations on the continent on this special day. It transcends time as well, as evidenced by the letters I read to you previously. Do you not think that if the early explorers were alive today, they would be just as interested in our sense of being here as theirs? They are indeed with us tonight in spirit, and they also would appreciate a place at the table. Please make room for them if you can.

And so, on this special evening, I propose a toast to all the Antarctic Heroes, past and present.

From My Midwinter 2013 at the South Pole I would like to add:

I have the privilege and honor of working in one of the most isolated places on Earth. Amundsen-Scott South Pole Station closed in early February leaving 44 souls to work and live in isolation for 9 months. The station will reopen in early November for the short Antarctic summer when the population swells to 150. During this time, we have been subjected to periods of brutal temperatures down to -107 F with winds that easily drop the temperature to under -140. At these temperatures, the word 'cold' doesn't mean anything. Even 'extremely cold' is not appropriate. There is no word to describe the feeling as you walk in the darkness and try to survive from one building to the next. If the weather conditions permit, you may see a faint red light where you are headed. The darkness along with the cold and wind can and will disorientate you in seconds; the large snow drifts will test your stamina, and frequent stumbling will make you think *Now which way was I headed?* as the last thing you want is to be lost. But when it is clear, the reward is simply stunning as the sky is filled with stars and varying shapes and colors of dazzling auroras that stretch from horizon to horizon. The South Pole winter sky is unmatched in beauty. They say that a successful Antarctic winter is when you return home with 10 fingers and 10 toes. This may sound funny, but believe me, it is so very true. So why am I here? It is probably one of the most unique opportunities on the planet to live an adventure, and it is a huge physical and mental challenge. This is only my second winter, and this "old Antarctic explorer" is enjoying the Antarctic experience.

Mike Rice 6-22-2013

Winter 2013 at the South Pole

The Father and Daughter
Bicycling Adventures will continue!

We are planning to leave for Lisbon, Portugal in March of 2014 to start a world-wide bicycling tour of Europe, Asia, and then from the tip of South America to Prudhoe Bay, Alaska. We will then cross Canada from Victoria, BC to New Brunswick and then ride south to our home in Cape Canaveral, Florida.

Contact information and links:

Mike mikey8590@gmail.com

Jocelyn jrice1017@gmail.com

Visit our website at: FatherDaughterCyclingAdventures.com

Both of the journeys in this book are in more detail and with hundreds of color pictures at crazyguyonabike.com/mikey8590

These journeys are also on Jocelyn's Facebook page "Believe the Ride". To find, Google - Believe the Ride Jocelyn Rice. You do not need to be a member of Facebook to view her page.

My Antarctic adventures are blogged at:

Mikeontheice.blogspot.com – McMurdo Station winter of 2012

Southpolemike.blogspot.com – South Pole winter of 2013

Dad…we kept the wheels going around and around once again.

"Twenty years from now you will be more disappointed by the things you didn't do than by the ones you did do. So throw off the bowlines. Sail away from the safe harbor. Catch the trade winds in your sails. Explore. Dream. Discover."

– Mark Twain

42747667R00141

Made in the USA
Lexington, KY
03 July 2015